THE SOLILOQUIES

THE
SOLILOQUIES

WILLIAM SHAKESPEARE

VIKING
an imprint of
PENGUIN BOOKS

Viking

Penguin Group (Australia)
250 Camberwell Road, Camberwell, Victoria 3124, Australia
Penguin Books Ltd
80 Strand, London WC2R 0RL, England
Penguin Group (USA) Inc.
375 Hudson Street, New York, New York 10014, USA
Penguin Books, a division of Pearson Canada
10 Alcorn Avenue, Toronto, Ontario, Canada M4V 3B2
Penguin Group (NZ)
cnr Airborne and Rosedale Roads, Albany, Auckland 1310, New Zealand
Penguin Books (South Africa) (Pty) Ltd
24 Sturdee Avenue, Rosebank, Johannesburg 2196, South Africa
Penguin Books India (P) Ltd
11, Community Centre, Panchsheel Park, New Delhi 110 017, India

First published by Penguin Group (Australia),
a division of Pearson Australia Group Pty Ltd, 2004

10 9 8 7 6 5 4 3 2 1

Design by Adam Laszczuk © Penguin Group (Australia)

Typeset in 10.5/14 pt Cochin by Post Pre-press Group
Printed in China by Everbest Printing Co Ltd

National Library of Australia
Cataloguing-in-Publication data:

Shakespeare, William 1564–1616.
[Plays. Selections.]
Shakespeare's soliloquies.

Includes index.
ISBN 0 670 04264 1.

1. Drama – Collections. I. Title.

822.33

www.penguin.com.au

CONTENTS

[II, iii, 1–30] *Lance, the servant-boy, is off on his travels with his master Proteus. All have been sad to see him go except his dog, Crab:*

Nay, 'twill be this hour ere I have done weeping; all the kind of the Launces have this very fault. I have received my proportion, like the prodigious son, and am going with Sir Proteus to the Imperial's court. I think Crab my dog be the sourest-natured dog that lives. My mother weeping, my father wailing, my sister crying, our maid howling, our cat wringing her hands, and all our house in a great perplexity; yet did not this cruel-hearted cur shed one tear. He is a stone, a very pebblestone, and has no more pity in him than a dog. A Jew would have wept to have seen our parting. Why, my grandam, having no eyes, look you, wept herself blind at my parting. Nay, I'll show you the manner of it. This shoe is my father. No, this left shoe is my father. No, no, left shoe is my mother. Nay, that cannot be so neither. Yes, it is so, it is so, it hath the worser sole. This shoe with the hole in it is my mother, and this my father. A vengeance on't, there 'tis. Now, sir, this staff is my sister; for, look you, she is as white as a lily and as small as a wand. This hat is Nan our maid. I am the dog. No, the dog is himself, and I am the dog. O, the dog is me, and I am myself. Ay, so, so. Now come I to my father: 'Father, your blessing.' Now should not the shoe speak a word for weeping. Now should I kiss my father; well, he weeps on. Now come

I to my mother. O, that she could speak now like an old woman! Well, I kiss her. Why, there 'tis; here's my mother's breath up and down. Now come I to my sister. Mark the moan she makes. Now the dog all this while sheds not a tear, nor speaks a word; but see how I lay the dust with my tears.

[II, iv, 190–212] *Proteus struggles to comprehend and justify his fickle feelings for his former love, Julia and his new love, Silvia:*

Even as one heat another heat expels,
  Or as one nail by strength drives out another,
So the remembrance of my former love
Is by a newer object quite forgotten.
Is it my mind, or Valentine's praise,
Her true perfection, or my false transgression,
That makes me reasonless to reason thus?
She is fair; and so is Julia that I love–
That I did love, for now my love is thawed;
Which, like a waxen image 'gainst a fire,
Bears no impression of the thing it was.
Methinks my zeal to Valentine is cold,
And that I love him not as I was wont.
O, but I love his lady too too much,
And that's the reason I love him so little.
How shall I dote on her with more advice
That thus without advice begin to love her!
'Tis but her picture I have yet beheld,
And that hath dazzlèd my reason's light;
But when I look on her perfections,

There is no reason but I shall be blind.
If I can check my erring love, I will;
If not, to compass her I'll use my skill.

[II, vi, 1–38] *As his passion deepens, so too does his confusion,*
Proteus seeks to balance the demands of love and loyalty:

To leave my Julia, shall I be forsworn;
  To love fair Silvia, shall I be forsworn;
To wrong my friend, I shall be much forsworn.
And e'en that power which gave me first my oath
Provokes me to this threefold perjury:
Love bade me swear, and Love bids me forswear.
O sweet-suggesting Love, if thou hast sinn'd,
Teach me, thy tempted subject, to excuse it!
At first I did adore a twinkling star,
But now I worship a celestial sun.
Unheedful vows may heedfully be broken;
And he wants wit that wants resolvèd will
To learn his wit t'exchange the bad for better.
Fie, fie, unreverend tongue, to call her bad
Whose sovereignty so oft thou hast preferred
With twenty thousand soul-confirming oaths!
I cannot leave to love, and yet I do;
But there I leave to love where I should love.
Julia I lose, and Valentine I lose;
If I keep them, I needs must lose myself;
If I lose them, thus find I by their loss:
For Valentine, myself; for Julia, Silvia.
I to myself am dearer than a friend,
For love is still most precious in itself;

And Silvia – witness heaven, that made her fair!–
Shows Julia but a swarthy Ethiope.
I will forget that Julia is alive,
Remembering that my love to her is dead;
And Valentine I'll hold an enemy,
Aiming at Silvia as a sweeter friend.
I cannot now prove constant to myself
Without some treachery used to Valentine.

[V, iv, 1–12] *Bruised by love, Valentine finds consolation in solitude:*

How use doth breed a habit in a man!
This shadowy desert, unfrequented woods,
I better brook than flourishing peopled towns.
Here can I sit alone, unseen of any,
And to the nightingale's complaining notes
Tune my distresses, and record my woes.
O thou that dost inhabit in my breast,
Leave not the mansion so long tenantless,
Lest, growing ruinous, the building fall
And leave no memory of what it was!
Repair me with thy presence, Silvia:
Thou gentle nymph, cherish thy forlorn swain.

[IV, i, 174–97] *Petruchio reveals his plan for taming Katherine:*

Thus have I politicly begun my reign,
    And 'tis my hope to end successfully.
My falcon now is sharp and passing empty,
And till she stoop she must not be full-gorged,
For then she never looks upon her lure.
Another way I have to man my haggard,
To make her come, and know her keeper's call,
That is, to watch her, as we watch these kites
That bate and beat and will not be obedient.
She eat no meat to-day, nor none shall eat.
Last night she slept not, nor tonight she shall not.
As with the meat, some undeservèd fault
I'll find about the making of the bed,
And here I'll fling the pillow, there the bolster,
This way the coverlet, another way the sheets.
Ay, and amid this hurly I intend
That all is done in reverend care of her.
And, in conclusion, she shall watch all night,
And if she chance to nod I'll rail and brawl,
And with the clamour keep her still awake.
This is a way to kill a wife with kindness,
And thus I'll curb her mad and headstrong humour.
He that knows better how to tame a shrew,
Now let him speak – 'tis charity to show.

[I, i, 212–57] Richard Plantagenet, Duke of York seethes with anger as he sees Henry VI waste the power and influence of the Crown he believes is rightfully his:

Anjou and Maine are given to the French;
Paris is lost; the state of Normandy
Stands on a tickle point now they are gone.
Suffolk concluded on the articles,
The peers agreed, and Henry was well pleased
To change two dukedoms for a duke's fair daughter.
I cannot blame them all; what is't to them?
'Tis thine they give away, and not their own.
Pirates may make cheap pennyworths of their pillage
And purchase friends and give to courtesans,
Still revelling like lords till all be gone;
While as the silly owner of the goods
Weeps over them, and wrings his hapless hands,
And shakes his head, and trembling stands aloof,
While all is shared and all is borne away,
Ready to starve, and dare not touch his own.
So York must sit and fret and bite his tongue,
While his own lands are bargained for and sold.
Methinks the realms of England, France, and Ireland,
Bear that proportion to my flesh and blood
As did the fatal brand Althaea burnt
Unto the prince's heart of Calydon.
Anjou and Maine both given unto the French!
Cold news for me; for I had hope of France,
Even as I have of fertile England's soil.

A day will come when York shall claim his own,
And therefore I will take the Nevils' parts
And make a show of love to proud Duke Humphrey,
And, when I spy advantage, claim the crown,
For that's the golden mark I seek to hit.
Nor shall proud Lancaster usurp my right,
Nor hold the sceptre in his childish fist,
Nor wear the diadem upon his head,
Whose church-like humours fits not for a crown.
Then, York, be still awhile, till time do serve;
Watch thou, and wake, when others be asleep,
To pry into the secrets of the state,
Till Henry, surfeiting in joys of love
With his new bride and England's dear-bought queen,
And Humphrey with the peers be fall'n at jars.
Then will I raise aloft the milk-white rose,
With whose sweet smell the air shall be perfumed,
And in my standard bear the arms of York,
To grapple with the house of Lancaster;
And force perforce I'll make them yield the crown,
Whose bookish rule hath pulled fair England down.

[III, i, 331–83] *York has been sent to Ireland to put down an insurrection, and to distance him from the English throne. But by furnishing him with an army, the King has supplied York with an opportunity to take action:*

Now, York, or never, steel thy fearful thoughts,
And change misdoubt to resolution;
Be that thou hopest to be, or what thou art
Resign to death; it is not worth th'enjoying.

Let pale-faced fear keep with the mean-born man,
And find no harbour in a royal heart.
Faster than spring-time showers comes thought on
    thought,
And not a thought but thinks on dignity.
My brain, more busy than the labouring spider,
Weaves tedious snares to trap mine enemies.
Well, nobles, well; 'tis politicly done,
To send me packing with an host of men.
I fear me you but warm the starvèd snake,
Who, cherished in your breasts, will sting your hearts.
'Twas men I lacked, and you will give them me;
I take it kindly; yet be well assured
You put sharp weapons in a madman's hands.
Whiles I in Ireland nourish a mighty band,
I will stir up in England some black storm
Shall blow ten thousand souls to heaven or hell;
And this fell tempest shall not cease to rage
Until the golden circuit on my head,
Like to the glorious sun's transparent beams,
Do calm the fury of this mad-bred flaw.
And, for a minister of my intent,
I have seduced a headstrong Kentishman,
John Cade of Ashford,
To make commotion, as full well he can,
Under the tide of John Mortimer.
In Ireland have I seen this stubborn Cade
Oppose himself against a troop of kerns,
And fought so long till that his thighs with darts
Were almost like a sharp-quilled porpentine;
And, in the end being rescued, I have seen

Him caper upright like a wild Morisco,
Shaking the bloody darts as he his bells.
Full often, like a shag-haired crafty kern,
Hath he conversèd with the enemy,
And undiscovered come to me again
And given me notice of their villainies.
This devil here shall be my substitute;
For that John Mortimer, which now is dead,
In face, in gait, in speech, he doth resemble;
By this I shall perceive the commons' mind,
How they affect the house and claim of York.
Say he be taken, racked, and torturèd,
I know no pain they can inflict upon him
Will make him say I moved him to those arms.
Say that he thrive, as 'tis great like he will,
Why, then from Ireland come I with my strength,
And reap the harvest which that rascal sowed;
For Humphrey being dead, as he shall be,
And Henry put apart, the next for me.

[I, iv, 1–26] *Seemingly poised for succession to the throne, a new obstacle faces York in the form of Queen Margaret. York has met this formidable opponent in battle, and it seems things are not going his way:*

The army of the Queen hath got the field;
  My uncles both are slain in rescuing me;
And all my followers to the eager foe
Turn back and fly, like ships before the wind
Or lambs pursued by hunger-starvèd wolves.
My sons, God knows what hath bechancèd them;
But this I know, they have demeaned themselves
Like men born to renown by life or death.
Three times did Richard make a lane to me,
And thrice cried 'Courage, father! Fight it out!'
And full as oft came Edward to my side,
With purple falchion, painted to the hilt
In blood of those that had encountered him.
And when the hardiest warriors did retire,
Richard cried 'Charge! And give no foot of ground!'
And cried 'A crown, or else a glorious tomb!
A sceptre or an earthly sepulchre!'
With this we charged again; but, out, alas!
We budged again; as I have seen a swan
With bootless labour swim against the tide
And spend her strength with overmatching waves.
    A short alarum within
Ah, hark! The fatal followers do pursue,
And I am faint and cannot fly their fury;

And were I strong, I would not shun their fury.
The sands are numbered that make up my life;
Here must I stay, and here my life must end.

[II, v, 1–54] *Henry VI is more inclined to philosophy than battle:*

This battle fares like to the morning's war,
    When dying clouds contend with growing light,
What time the shepherd, blowing of his nails,
Can neither call it perfect day nor night.
Now sways it this way, like a mighty sea
Forced by the tide to combat with the wind;
Now sways it that way, like the self-same sea
Forced to retire by fury of the wind.
Sometime the flood prevails, and then the wind;
Now one the better, then another best;
Both tugging to be victors, breast to breast,
Yet neither conqueror nor conquerèd;
So is the equal poise of this fell war.
Here on this molehill will I sit me down.
To whom God will, there be the victory!
For Margaret my Queen, and Clifford too,
Have chid me from the battle, swearing both
They prosper best of all when I am thence.
Would I were dead, if God's good will were so!
For what is in this world but grief and woe?
O God! Methinks it were a happy life
To be no better than a homely swain;
To sit upon a hill, as I do now;
To carve out dials quaintly, point by point,
Thereby to see the minutes how they run:

How many makes the hour full complete,
How many hours brings about the day,
How many days will finish up the year,
How many years a mortal man may live.
When this is known, then to divide the times:
So many hours must I tend my flock,
So many hours must I take my rest,
So many hours must I contemplate,
So many hours must I sport myself,
So many days my ewes have been with young,
So many weeks ere the poor fools will ean,
So many years ere I shall shear the fleece.
So minutes, hours, days, months, and years,
Passed over to the end they were created,
Would bring white hairs unto a quiet grave.
Ah, what a life were this! How sweet! How lovely!
Gives not the hawthorn bush a sweeter shade
To shepherds looking on their silly sheep
Than doth a rich embroidered canopy
To kings that fear their subjects' treachery?
O yes, it doth; a thousand-fold it doth.
And to conclude: the shepherd's homely curds,
His cold thin drink out of his leather bottle,
His wonted sleep under a fresh tree's shade,
All which secure and sweetly he enjoys,
Is far beyond a prince's delicates,
His viands sparkling in a golden cup,
His body couchèd in a curious bed,
When care, mistrust, and treason waits on him.

[II, v, 55–124] *Soldiers enter bearing the bodies of men they have slain. The King retires, and a heartbreaking three part soliloquy follows:*

SON

I ll blows the wind that profits nobody.
This man whom hand to hand I slew in fight
May be possessèd with some store of crowns;
And I, that haply take them from him now,
May yet ere night yield both my life and them
To some man else, as this dead man doth me. –
        Takes off dead man's helmet
Who's this? O God! It is my father's face,
Whom in this conflict, I, unwares, have killed.
O, heavy times, begetting such events!
From London by the King was I pressed forth;
My father, being the Earl of Warwick's man,
Came on the part of York, pressed by his master;
And I, who at his hands received my life,
Have by my hands of life bereavèd him.
Pardon me, God, I knew not what I did!
And pardon, father, for I knew not thee!
My tears shall wipe away these bloody marks;
And no more words till they have flowed their fill.

KING

O, piteous spectacle! O, bloody times!
Whiles lions war and battle for their dens,
Poor harmless lambs abide their enmity.
Weep, wretched man; I'll aid thee tear for tear;
And let our hearts and eyes, like civil war,
Be blind with tears and break o'ercharged with grief.

Enter at another door a Father that hath killed his son,
with the dead body in his arms

FATHER

Thou that so stoutly hath resisted me,
Give me thy gold, if thou hast any gold;
For I have bought it with an hundred blows.
But let me see: is this our foeman's face?
Ah, no, no, no, it is mine only son!
Ah, boy, if any life be left in thee,
Throw up thine eye! See, see what showers arise,
Blown with the windy tempest of my heart,
Upon thy wounds, that kills mine eye and heart!
O, pity, God, this miserable age!
What stratagems, how fell, how butcherly,
Erroneous, mutinous, and unnatural,
This deadly quarrel daily doth beget!
O boy, thy father gave thee life too soon,
And hath bereft thee of thy life too late!

KING

Woe above woe! Grief more than common grief!
O that my death would stay these ruthful deeds!
O pity, pity, gentle heaven, pity!
The red rose and the white are on his face,
The fatal colours of our striving houses;
The one his purple blood right well resembles;
The other his pale cheeks, methinks, presenteth.
Wither one rose, and let the other flourish!
If you contend, a thousand lives must perish.

SON

How will my mother for a father's death
Take on with me, and ne'er be satisfied!

FATHER

How will my wife for slaughter of my son
Shed seas of tears, and ne'er be satisfied!

KING

How will the country for these woeful chances
Misthink the King, and not be satisfied!

SON

Was ever son so rued a father's death?

FATHER

Was ever father so bemoaned his son?

KING

Was ever king so grieved for subjects' woe?
Much is your sorrow; mine ten times so much.

SON

I'll bear thee hence, where I may weep my fill.

   Exit with the body of his father

FATHER

These arms of mine shall be thy winding-sheet;
My heart, sweet boy, shall be thy sepulchre,
For from my heart thine image ne'er shall go;
My sighing breast shall be thy funeral bell;
And so obsequious will thy father be,
Even for the loss of thee, having no more,
As Priam was for all his valiant sons.
I'll bear thee hence; and let them fight that will,
For I have murdered where I should not kill.

   Exit with the body of his son

KING

Sad-hearted men, much overgone with care,
Here sits a king more woeful than you are.

[III, ii, 124–95] *Richard, the Duke of Gloucester, broods on his brother's gracious and handsome ways as he views Edward's offspring as obstacles to his own line to the throne:*

Ay, Edward will use women honourably.
Would he were wasted, marrow, bones, and all,
That from his loins no hopeful branch may spring,
To cross me from the golden time I look for!
And yet, between my soul's desire and me –
The lustful Edward's title burièd –
Is Clarence, Henry, and his son young Edward,
And all the unlooked-for issue of their bodies,
To take their rooms ere I can place myself:
A cold premeditation for my purpose!
Why, then I do but dream on sovereignty;
Like one that stands upon a promontory
And spies a far-off shore where he would tread,
Wishing his foot were equal with his eye,
And chides the sea that sunders him from thence,
Saying he'll lade it dry to have his way;
So do I wish the crown, being so far off;
And so I chide the means that keeps me from it;
And so I say I'll cut the causes off,
Flattering me with impossibilities.
My eye's too quick, my heart o'erweens too much,
Unless my hand and strength could equal them.
Well, say there is no kingdom then for Richard,
What other pleasure can the world afford?
I'll make my heaven in a lady's lap,
And deck my body in gay ornaments,
And 'witch sweet ladies with my words and looks.

O, miserable thought! And more unlikely
Than to accomplish twenty golden crowns!
Why, love forswore me in my mother's womb;
And, for I should not deal in her soft laws,
She did corrupt frail nature with some bribe
To shrink mine arm up like a withered shrub;
To make an envious mountain on my back,
Where sits deformity to mock my body;
To shape my legs of an unequal size;
To disproportion me in every part,
Like to a chaos, or an unlicked bear-whelp
That carries no impression like the dam.
And am I then a man to be beloved?
O, monstrous fault, to harbour such a thought!
Then, since this earth affords no joy to me
But to command, to check, to o'erbear such
As are of better person than myself,
I'll make my heaven to dream upon the crown,
And whiles I live, t'account this world but hell,
Until my misshaped trunk that bear this head
Be round impalèd with a glorious crown,
And yet I know not how to get the crown,
For many lives stand between me and home;
And I – like one lost in a thorny wood,
That rents the thorns and is rent with the thorns,
Seeking a way and straying from the way,
Not knowing how to find the open air,
But toiling desperately to find it out –
Torment myself to catch the English crown;
And from that torment I will free myself,
Or hew my way out with a bloody axe.

Why, I can smile, and murder whiles I smile,
And cry 'Content!' to that which grieves my heart,
And wet my cheeks with artificial tears,
And frame my face to all occasions.
I'll drown more sailors than the mermaid shall;
I'll slay more gazers than the basilisk;
I'll play the orator as well as Nestor,
Deceive more slily than Ulysses could,
And, like a Sinon, take another Troy.
I can add colours to the chameleon,
Change shapes with Proteus for advantages,
And set the murderous Machiavel to school.
Can I do this, and cannot get a crown?
Tut, were it farther off, I'll pluck it down.

[V, vi, 61–93] *Unconcerned by the corporeal barriers to his
successon, Richard persists in his bloody path to power via the
cold-hearted murder of King Henry:*

What! Will the aspiring blood of Lancaster
    Sink in the ground? I thought it would have
        mounted.
See how my sword weeps for the poor King's death!
O, may such purple tears be always shed
From those that wish the downfall of our house!
If any spark of life be yet remaining,
Down, down to hell; and say I sent thee thither,
        (*He stabs him again*)
I that have neither pity, love, nor fear.
Indeed, 'tis true that Henry told me of;
For I have often heard my mother say

I came into the world with my legs forward.
Had I not reason, think ye, to make haste
And seek their ruin that usurped our right?
The midwife wondered and the women cried
'O, Jesus bless us, he is born with teeth!'
And so I was, which plainly signified
That I should snarl, and bite, and play the dog.
Then, since the heavens have shaped my body so,
Let hell make crooked my mind to answer it.
I have no brother, I am like no brother;
And this word 'love', which greybeards call divine,
Be resident in men like one another,
And not in me; I am myself alone.
Clarence, beware; thou keepest me from the light,
But I will sort a pitchy day for thee;
For I will buzz abroad such prophecies
That Edward shall be fearful of his life,
And then to purge his fear, I'll be thy death.
King Henry and the Prince his son are gone;
Clarence, thy turn is next, and then the rest,
Counting myself but bad till I be best.
I'll throw thy body in another room,
And triumph, Henry, in thy day of doom.

TITUS ANDRONICUS

[II, i, 1—24] *The servant Aaron sees the marriage of his lover Tamora, the Gothic Queen, as an opportunity to gain power:*

Now climbeth Tamora Olympus' top,
    Safe out of fortune's shot, and sits aloft,
Secure of thunder's crack or lightning flash,
Advanc'd above pale envy's threat'ning reach.
As when the golden sun salutes the morn
And, having gilt the ocean with his beams,
Gallops the zodiac in his glistening coach
And overlooks the highest-peering hills,
So Tamora.
Upon her wit doth earthly honour wait,
And virtue stoops and trembles at her frown.
Then, Aaron, arm thy heart and fit thy thoughts
To mount aloft with thy imperial mistress,
And mount her pitch, whom thou in triumph long
Hast prisoner held, fettered in amorous chains,
And faster bound to Aaron's charming eyes
Than is Prometheus tied to Caucasus.
Away with slavish weeds and servile thoughts!
I will be bright and shine in pearl and gold,
To wait upon this new-made Emperess.
'To wait' said I? – to wanton with this queen,
This goddess, this Semiramis, this nymph,
This siren that will charm Rome's Saturnine,
And see his shipwreck and his commonweal's.

[I, v, 19–26] *Lord Talbot is awed by what he sees as the fiendish skill of Joan of Arc:*

My thoughts are whirlèd like a potter's wheel;
I know not where I am nor what I do.
A witch by fear, not force, like Hannibal,
Drives back our troops and conquers as she lists.
So bees with smoke and doves with noisome stench
Are from their hives and houses driven away.
They called us, for our fierceness, English dogs;
Now, like to whelps, we crying run away . . .

[IV, i, 182–94] *While impressed by Richard's restraint in the face of King Henry's feeble rule, Exeter wonders how long the rivalries between England's noble houses will remain in check:*

Well didst thou, Richard, to suppress thy voice;
For had the passions of thy heart burst out,
I fear we should have seen deciphered there
More rancorous spite, more furious raging broils,
Than yet can be imagined or supposed.
But howsoe'er, no simple man that sees
This jarring discord of nobility,
This shouldering of each other in the court,
This factious bandying of their favourites,
But that it doth presage some ill event.
'Tis much when sceptres are in children's hands;
But more when envy breeds unkind division:
There comes the ruin, there begins confusion.

RICHARD III

[I, i, 1–40] *Richard's family has realised the power he so desperately sought, despite this Richard feels more an outsider than ever at the moment of his brother Edward's success:*

Now is the winter of our discontent
Made glorious summer by this sun of York,
And all the clouds that loured upon our house
In the deep bosom of the ocean buried.
Now are our brows bound with victorious wreaths;
Our bruisèd arms hung up for monuments,
Our stern alarums chang'd to merry meetings,
Our dreadful marches to delightful measures.
Grim-visaged war hath smoothed his wrinkled front,
And now, instead of mounting barbèd steeds
To fright the souls of fearful adversaries,
He capers nimbly in a lady's chamber
To the lascivious pleasing of a lute.
But I, that am not shaped for sportive tricks
Nor made to court an amorous looking-glass;
I, that am rudely stamped, and want love's majesty
To strut before a wanton ambling nymph;
I, that am curtailed of this fair proportion,
Cheated of feature by dissembling Nature,
Deformed, unfinished, sent before my time
Into this breathing world scarce half made up,
And that so lamely and unfashionable
That dogs bark at me as I halt by them –
Why, I, in this weak piping time of peace,
Have no delight to pass away the time,

Unless to spy my shadow in the sun
And descant on mine own deformity.
And therefore, since I cannot prove a lover
To entertain these fair well-spoken days,
I am determined to prove a villain
And hate the idle pleasures of these days.
Plots have I laid, inductions dangerous,
By drunken prophecies, libels, and dreams,
To set my brother Clarence and the King
In deadly hate the one against the other;
And if King Edward be as true and just
As I am subtle, false, and treacherous,
This day should Clarence closely be mewed up
About a prophecy which says that G
Of Edward's heirs the murderer shall be.

[I, ii, 227–63] *Equally obsessed with sexual and political power,
Richard relishes the hold he believes he has over Lady Anne:*

Was ever woman in this humour wooed?
  Was ever woman in this humour won?
I'll have her, but I will not keep her long.
What? I that killed her husband and his father
To take her in her heart's extremest hate,
With curses in her mouth, tears in her eyes,
The bleeding witness of my hatred by,
Having God, her conscience, and these bars against me,
And I no friends to back my suit at all
But the plain devil and dissembling looks?
And yet to win her! All the world to nothing!
Ha!

Hath she forgot already that brave prince,
Edward, her lord, whom I, some three months since,
Stabbed in my angry mood at Tewkesbury?
A sweeter and a lovelier gentleman,
Framed in the prodigality of nature,
Young, valiant, wise, and, no doubt, right royal,
The spacious world cannot again afford;
And will she yet abase her eyes on me,
That cropped the golden prime of this sweet prince
And made her widow to a woeful bed?
On me, whose all not equals Edward's moiety?
On me, that halts and am misshapen thus?
My dukedom to a beggarly denier
I do mistake my person all this while!
Upon my life, she finds, although I cannot,
Myself to be a marvellous proper man.
I'll be at charges for a looking-glass
And entertain a score or two of tailors
To study fashions to adorn my body.
Since I am crept in favour with myself
I will maintain it with some little cost.
But first I'll turn yon fellow in his grave,
And then return lamenting to my love.
Shine out, fair sun, till I have bought a glass,
That I may see my shadow as I pass.

[V, iii, 178–207] *Haunted by the ghosts of his victims,
Richard fears for his soul:*

Give me another horse! Bind up my wounds!
Have mercy, Jesu! – Soft! I did but dream.

O coward conscience, how dost thou afflict me!
The lights burn blue. It is now dead midnight.
Cold fearful drops stand on my trembling flesh.
What do I fear? Myself? There's none else by.
Richard loves Richard: that is, I am I.
Is there a murderer here? No. Yes, I am.
Then fly. What, from myself? Great reason why –
Lest I revenge. Myself upon myself?
Alack, I love myself. Wherefore? For any good
That I myself have done unto myself?
O, no! Alas, I rather hate myself
For hateful deeds committed by myself!
I am a villain. Yet I lie, I am not.
Fool, of thyself speak well. Fool, do not flatter.
My conscience hath a thousand several tongues,
And every tongue brings in a several tale,
And every tale condemns me for a villain.
Perjury, perjury, in the highest degree.
Murder, stern murder, in the direst degree.
All several sins, all used in each degree,
Throng to the bar, crying all 'Guilty! Guilty!'
I shall despair. There is no creature loves me;
And if I die, no soul will pity me.
Nay, wherefore should they, since that I myself
Find in myself no pity to myself?
Methought the souls of all that I had murdered
Came to my tent, and every one did threat
Tomorrow's vengeance on the head of Richard.

LOVE'S LABOUR'S LOST

[III, i, 170–202] *A cynic when it comes to Love, Berowne is bewildered when he is struck by Cupid's arrow:*

And I, forsooth, in love!
I, that have been love's whip,
A very beadle to a humorous sigh;
A critic, nay, a night-watch constable,
A domineering pedant o'er the boy,
Than whom no mortal so magnificent!
This wimpled, whining, purblind, wayward boy,
This Signor Junior, giant-dwarf, Dan Cupid,
Regent of love-rhymes, lord of folded arms,
Th' anointed sovereign of sighs and groans,
Liege of all loiterers and malcontents,
Dread prince of plackets, king of codpieces,
Sole imperator and great general
Of trotting paritors – O my little heart!
And I to be a corporal of his field,
And wear his colours like a tumbler's hoop!
What? I love? I sue? I seek a wife?
A woman, that is like a German clock,
Still a-repairing, ever out of frame,
And never going aright, being a watch,
But being watched that it may still go right!
Nay, to be perjured, which is worst of all;
And, among three, to love the worst of all –
A whitely wanton with a velvet brow,
With two pitch-balls stuck in her face for eyes;
Ay, and, by heaven, one that will do the deed,

Though Argus were her eunuch and her guard!
And I to sigh for her, to watch for her,
To pray for her! Go to, it is a plague
That Cupid will impose for my neglect
Of his almighty dreadful little might.
Well, I will love, write, sigh, pray, sue, and groan;
Some men must love my lady, and some Joan.

A MIDSUMMER NIGHT'S DREAM

[I, i, 226–45] *Helena contemplates the fickleness of love as she realises Demetrius has shifted his affections to Hermia:*

How happy some o'er other some can be!
Through Athens I am thought as fair as she.
But what of that? Demetrius thinks not so;
He will not know what all but he do know.
And as he errs, doting on Hermia's eyes,
So I, admiring of his qualities.
Things base and vile, holding no quantity,
Love can transpose to form and dignity.
Love looks not with the eyes, but with the mind,
And therefore is winged Cupid painted blind.
Nor hath love's mind of any judgement taste;
Wings and no eyes figure unheedy haste.
And therefore is love said to be a child
Because in choice he is so oft beguiled.
As waggish boys in game themselves forswear,
So the boy love is perjured everywhere;
For ere Demetrius looked on Hermia's eyne,
He hailed down oaths that he was only mine,
And when this hail some heat from Hermia felt,
So he dissolved, and showers of oaths did melt.

[II, ii, 2–25] *As Romeo star-gazes, he rails against Diana the moon-goddess and patron of chastity:*

B ut soft! What light through yonder window
      breaks?
It is the East, and Juliet is the sun!
Arise, fair sun, and kill the envious moon,
Who is already sick and pale with grief
That thou her maid art far more fair than she.
Be not her maid, since she is envious.
Her vestal livery is but sick and green,
And none but fools do wear it. Cast it off.
It is my lady. O, it is my love!
O that she knew she were!
She speaks. Yet she says nothing. What of that?
Her eye discourses. I will answer it.
I am too bold. 'Tis not to me she speaks.
Two of the fairest stars in all the heaven,
Having some business, do entreat her eyes
To twinkle in their spheres till they return.
What if her eyes were there, they in her head?
The brightness of her cheek would shame those stars
As daylight doth a lamp. Her eyes in heaven
Would through the airy region stream so bright
That birds would sing and think it were not night.
See how she leans her cheek upon her hand!
O that I were a glove upon that hand,
That I might touch that cheek!

[II, ii, 33–49] *Thinking she is alone, Juliet speaks her heart,
only to be overheard by Romeo:*

O Romeo, Romeo! – wherefore art thou Romeo?
  Deny thy father and refuse thy name.
Or, if thou wilt not, be but sworn my love,
And I'll no longer be a Capulet.
ROMEO (*aside*)
Shall I hear more, or shall I speak at this?
JULIET
'Tis but thy name that is my enemy.
Thou art thyself, though not a Montague.
What's Montague? It is nor hand, nor foot
Nor arm, nor face, nor any other part
Belonging to a man. O, be some other name!
What's in a name? That which we call a rose
By any other name would smell as sweet.
So Romeo would, were he not Romeo called,
Retain that dear perfection which he owes
Without that title, Romeo, doff thy name;
And for that name, which is no part of thee,
Take all myself.

[III, ii, 1–31] *Impatient to see her lover, Juliet urges on the
setting sun, longing for the arrival of night, and Romeo:*

G allop apace, you fiery-footed steeds,
  Towards Phoebus' lodging! Such a waggoner
As Phaëton would whip you to the West
And bring in cloudy night immediately.
Spread thy close curtain, love-performing night,

That runaway's eyes may wink, and Romeo
Leap to these arms untalked of and unseen.
Lovers can see to do their amorous rites
By their own beauties; or, if love be blind,
It best agrees with night. Come, civil night,
Thou sober-suited matron, all in black,
And learn me how to lose a winning match,
Played for a pair of stainless maidenhoods.
Hood my unmanned blood, bating in my cheeks,
With thy black mantle till strange love, grown bold,
Think true love acted simple modesty.
Come, night. Come, Romeo. Come, thou day in night;
For thou wilt lie upon the wings of night
Whiter than new snow upon a raven's back.
Come, gentle night. Come, loving, black-browed night.
Give me my Romeo. And when I shall die,
Take him and cut him out in little stars,
And he will make the face of heaven so fine
That all the world will be in love with night
And pay no worship to the garish sun.
O I have bought the mansion of a love,
But not possessed it; and though I am sold,
Not yet enjoyed. So tedious is this day
As is the night before some festival
To an impatient child that hath new robes
And may not wear them.

[V, v, 1–6] *Once a King, now a prisoner, Richard struggles to find an apt metaphor for his altered state:*

I have been studying how I may compare
This prison where I live unto the world;
And, for because the world is populous,
And here is not a creature but myself,
I cannot do it. Yet I'll hammer it out.
My brain I'll prove the female to my soul,
My soul the father; and these two beget
A generation of still-breeding thoughts,
And these same thoughts people this little world,
In humours like the people of this world,
For no thought is contented; the better sort,
As thoughts of things divine, are intermixed
With scruples, and do set the word itself
Against the word, as thus: 'Come, little ones';
And then again,
'It is as hard to come as for a camel
To thread the postern of a small needle's eye.'
Thoughts tending to ambition, they do plot
Unlikely wonders – how these vain weak nails
May tear a passage through the flinty ribs
Of this hard world, my ragged prison walls,
And for they cannot, die in their own pride.
Thoughts tending to content flatter themselves
That they are not the first of Fortune's slaves,
Nor shall not be the last; like seely beggars
Who, sitting in the stocks, refuge their shame

That many have and others must sit there.
And in this thought they find a kind of ease,
Bearing their own misfortunes on the back
Of such as have before endured the like.
Thus play I in one person many people,
And none contented. Sometimes am I king;
Then treasons make me wish myself a beggar;
And so I am. Then crushing penury
Persuades me I was better when a king.
Then am I kinged again; and by and by
Think that I am unkinged by Bolingbroke,
And straight am nothing. But whate'er I be,
Nor I, nor any man that but man is,
With nothing shall be pleased till he be eased
With being nothing. (*The music plays*) Music do I hear.
Ha, ha; keep time. How sour sweet music is
When time is broke and no proportion kept.
So is it in the music of men's lives;
And here have I the daintiness of ear
To check time broke in a disordered string,
But for the concord of my state and time,
Had not an ear to hear my true time broke.
I wasted time, and now doth time waste me;
For now hath time made me his numbering clock.
My thoughts are minutes, and with sighs they jar
Their watches on unto mine eyes, the outward watch
Whereto my finger, like a dial's point,
Is pointing still in cleansing them from tears.
Now, sir, the sound that tells what hour it is
Are clamorous groans which strike upon my heart,
Which is the bell. So sighs, and tears, and groans

Show minutes, times, and hours. But my time
Runs posting on in Bolingbroke's proud joy,
While I stand fooling here, his jack of the clock.
This music mads me. Let it sound no more;
For though it have holp madman to their wits,
In me it seems it will make wise men mad.
Yet blessing on his heart that gives it me;
For 'tis a sign of love; and love to Richard
Is a strange brooch in this all-hating world.

KING JOHN

[II, i, 561–98] As the bastard-son of Richard I, Philip Falconbridge occupies a position outside of power. From this vantage-point he observes the machinations of a world motivated by personal advantage:

M ad world! Mad kings! Mad composition!
John, to stop Arthur's title in the whole,
Hath willingly departed with a part;
And France, whose armour conscience buckled on,
Whom zeal and charity brought to the field
As God's own soldier, rounded in the ear
With that same purpose-changer, that sly devil,
That broker that still breaks the pate of faith,
That daily break-vow, he that wins of all,
Of kings, of beggars, old men, young men, maids –
Who, having no external thing to lose
But the word 'maid', cheats the poor maid of that –
That smooth-faced gentleman, tickling commodity;
Commodity, the bias of the world –
The world, who of itself is peisèd well,
Made to run even upon even ground,
Till this advantage, this vile-drawing bias,
This sway of motion, this commodity,
Makes it take head from all indifferency,
From all direction, purpose, course, intent –
And this same bias, this commodity,
This bawd, this broker, this all-changing word,
Clapped on the outward eye of fickle France,
Hath drawn him from his own determined aid,

From a resolved and honourable war,
To a most base and vile-concluded peace.
And why rail I on this commodity?
But for because he hath not wooed me yet;
Not that I have the power to clutch my hand
When his fair angels would salute my palm,
But for my hand, as unattempted yet,
Like a poor beggar raileth on the rich,
Well, whiles I am a beggar, I will rail
And say there is no sin but to be rich;
And being rich, my virtue then shall be
To say there is no vice but beggary.
Since kings break faith upon commodity,
Gain, be my lord – for I will worship thee.

HENRY IV PART 1

[I, ii, 193–215] *Prince Harry tells his cohorts he believes the more reckless and debauched his life, the greater the glory when he changes his reprobate ways:*

I know you all, and will awhile uphold
The unyoked humour of your idleness.
Yet herein will I imitate the sun,
Who doth permit the base contagious clouds
To smother up his beauty from the world,
That, when he please again to be himself,
Being wanted, he may be more wondered at
By breaking through the foul and ugly mists
Of vapours that did seem to strangle him.
If all the year were playing holidays,
To sport would be as tedious as to work;
But when they seldom come, they wished-for come,
And nothing pleaseth but rare accidents.
So, when this loose behaviour I throw off,
And pay the debt I never promisèd,
By how much better than my word I am,
By so much shall I falsify men's hopes;
And, like bright metal on a sullen ground,
My reformation, glittering o'er my fault,
Shall show more goodly and attract more eyes
Than that which hath no foil to set it off.
I'll so offend to make offence a skill,
Redeeming time when men think least I will.

[V, i, 127–40] *Prince Harry has told Sir John Falstaff that he owes God a death, but John makes it clear he has no intention of repaying the debt on the battlefield:*

'Tis not due yet – I would be loath to pay him before his day. What need I be so forward with him that calls not on me? Well, 'tis no matter, honour pricks me on. Yea, but how if honour prick me off when I come on, how then? Can honour set to a leg? No. Or an arm? No. Or take away the grief of a wound? No. Honour hath no skill in surgery then? No. What is honour? A word. What is that word honour? Air. A trim reckoning! Who hath it? He that died a' Wednesday. Doth he feel it? No. Doth he hear it? No. 'Tis insensible then? Yea, to the dead. But will it not live with the living? No. Why? Detraction will not suffer it. Therefore I'll none of it. Honour is a mere scutcheon – and so ends my catechism.

[V, iv, 86–109] *Prince Harry's glorious victory is tempered by the sight of the dead body of his drinking companion Falstaff:*

For worms, brave Percy. Fare thee well, great heart!
Ill-weaved ambition, how much art thou shrunk.
When that this body did contain a spirit,
A kingdom for it was too small a bound;
But now two paces of the vilest earth
Is room enough. This earth that bears thee dead
Bears not alive so stout a gentleman.
If thou wert sensible of courtesy

I should not make so dear a show of zeal,
But let my favours hide thy mangled face,
And even in thy behalf I'll thank myself
For doing these fair rites of tenderness.
Adieu, and take thy praise with thee to heaven!
Thy ignominy sleep with thee in the grave,
But not remembered in thy epitaph!
    (*He spieth Falstaff on the ground*)
What, old acquaintance, could not all this flesh
Keep in a little life? Poor Jack, farewell!
I could have better spared a better man.
O, I should have a heavy miss of thee
If I were much in love with vanity.
Death hath not struck so fat a deer today,
Though many dearer, in this bloody fray.
Embowelled will I see thee by and by;
Till then in blood by noble Percy lie.

[V, iv, 110–27] *Yet Falstaff is not dead, as Harry leaves, he rises
to deliver a heroic response:*

Embowelled? If thou embowel me to-day, I'll give
you leave to powder me and eat me too tomorrow.
'Sblood, 'twas time to counterfeit, or that hot termagant
Scot had paid me, scot and lot too. Counterfeit? I lie,
I am no counterfeit. To die is to be a counterfeit, for
he is but the counterfeit of a man who hath not the
life of a man. But to counterfeit dying, when a man
thereby liveth, is to be no counterfeit, but the true and
perfect image of life indeed. The better part of valour is
discretion, in the which better part I have saved my

life. Zounds, I am afraid of this gunpowder Percy, though he be dead. How if he should counterfeit too, and rise? By my faith, I am afraid he would prove the better counterfeit. Therefore I'll make him sure, yea, and I'll swear I killed him. Why may not he rise as well as I? Nothing confutes me but eyes, and nobody sees me. therefore, sirrah (*stabbing him*), with a new wound in your thigh, come you along with me.

[III, i, 4–31] *King Henry, beleaguered by rebellions and an idle son, contemplates the responsibilities of office:*

How many thousands of my poorest subjects
    Are at this hour asleep! O sleep, O gentle sleep,
Nature's soft nurse, how have I frighted thee,
That thou no more will weigh my eyelids down
And steep my senses in forgetfulness?
Why rather, sleep, liest thou in smoky cribs,
Upon uneasy pallets stretching thee,
And hushed with buzzing night-flies to thy slumber,
Than in the perfumed chambers of the great,
Under the canopies of costly state,
And lulled with sound of sweetest melody?
O thou dull god, why liest thou with the vile
In loathsome beds, and leavest the kingly couch
A watch-case or a common 'larum-bell?
Wilt thou upon the high and giddy mast
Seal up the ship-boy's eyes, and rock his brains
In cradle of the rude imperious surge,
And in the visitation of the winds,
Who take the ruffian billows by the top,
Curling their monstrous heads, and hanging them
With deafing clamour in the slippery clouds,
That with the hurly death itself awakes?
Canst thou, O partial sleep, give thy repose
To the wet sea-son in an hour so rude,
And in the calmest and most stillest night,
With all appliances and means to boot,

Deny it to a king? Then, happy low, lie down!
Uneasy lies the head that wears a crown.

[IV, ii, 85–122] *Sir John Falstaff doubts the veracity of the*
Duke of Lancaster's promise to put in a good word: he distrust
a man who does not drink:

I would you had but the wit; 'twere better than your
dukedom. Good faith, this same young sober-
blooded boy doth not love me, nor a man cannot make
him laugh – but that's no marvel, he drinks no wine.
There's never none of these demure boys come to any
proof, for thin drink doth so over-cool their blood, and
making many fish meals, that they fall into a kind of
male green-sickness; and then when they marry they
get wenches. They are generally fools and cowards –
which some of us should be too, but for inflammation.
A good sherris-sack hath a two-fold operation in it. It
ascends me into the brain, dries me there all the foolish
and dull and crudy vapours which environ it, makes it
apprehensive, quick, forgetive, full of nimble, fiery, and
delectable shapes, which delivered o'er to the voice,
the tongue, which is the birth, becomes excellent wit.
The second property of your excellent sherris is the
warming of the blood, which before, cold and settled,
left the liver white and pale, which is the badge of
pusillanimity and cowardice; but the sherris warms
it, and makes it course from the inwards to the parts'
extremes. It illumineth the face, which, as a beacon,
gives warning to all the rest of this little kingdom, man,
to arm; and then the vital commoners and inland petty

spirits, muster me all to their captain, the heart, who,
great and puff'd up with this retinue, doth any deed of
courage; and this valour comes of sherris. So that skill
in the weapon is nothing without sack, for that sets
it a-work, and learning, a mere hoard of gold kept by
a devil, till sack commences it and sets it in act and use.
Hereof comes it that Prince Harry is valiant; for the
cold blood he did naturally inherit of his father he hath
like lean, sterile, and bare land, manured, husbanded,
and tilled, with excellent endeavour of drinking good
and good store of fertile sherris, that he is become
very hot and valiant. If I had a thousand sons, the
first human principle I would teach them should be to
forswear thin potations, and to addict themselves
to sack.

[IV, v, 22–48] *As he sits vigil at his dying father's bedside, Prince
Harry contemplates his destiny:*

W hy doth the crown lie there upon his pillow,
    Being so troublesome a bedfellow?
O polished perturbation! Golden care!
That keepest the ports of slumber open wide
To many a watchful night! Sleep with it now!
Yet not so sound, and half so deeply sweet,
As he whose brow with homely biggen bound
Snores out the watch of night. O majesty!
When thou dost pinch thy bearer, thou dost sit
Like a rich armour worn in heat of day,
That scaldest with safety. By his gates of breath
There lies a downy feather which stirs not;

Did he suspire, that light and weightless down
Perforce must move. My gracious lord! My father!
This sleep is sound indeed; this is a sleep
That from this golden rigol hath divorced
So many English kings. Thy due from me
Is tears and heavy sorrows of the blood,
Which nature, love, and filial tenderness,
Shall, O dear father, pay thee plenteously.
My due from thee is this imperial crown,
Which, as immediate from thy place and blood,
Derives itself to me. (*He puts the crown on his head*) Lo
    where it sits,
Which God shall guard, and put the world's whole
    strength
Into one giant arm, it shall not force
This lineal honour from me. This from thee
Will I to mine leave as 'tis left to me.

[II, iii, 8–33] *Protected from Cupid's arrows by his armour of scorn, Benedick ponders the mysterious powers of love and their impact on his friend Claudio:*

I do much wonder that one man, seeing how much another man is a fool when he dedicates his behaviours to love, will, after he hath laughed at such shallow follies in others, become the argument of his own scorn by falling in love; and such a man is Claudio. I have known when there was no music with him but the drum and the fife, and now had he rather hear the tabor and the pipe. I have known when he would have walked ten mile afoot to see a good armour, and now will he lie ten nights awake carving the fashion of a new doublet. He was wont to speak plain and to the purpose, like an honest man and a soldier, and now is he turned orthography; his words are a very fantastical banquet, just so many strange dishes. May I be so converted and see with these eyes? I cannot tell; I think not. I will not be sworn but love may transform me to an oyster; but I'll take my oath on it, till he have made an oyster of me he shall never make me such a fool. One woman is fair, yet I am well; another is wise, yet I am well; another virtuous, yet I am well; but till all graces be in one woman, one woman shall not come in my grace. Rich she shall be, that's certain; wise, or I'll none; virtuous, or I'll never cheapen her; fair, or I'll never look on her; mild, or come not near me; noble, or not I for an angel; of good discourse, an excellent musician, and her hair shall be of what colour it please God.

[IV, i, 223–77] *King Henry ponders the responsibilities of his rank:*

U pon the King! Let us our lives, our souls,
　　Our debts, our careful wives,
Our children, and our sins, lay on the King!
We must bear all. O hard condition,
Twin-born with greatness, subject to the breath
Of every fool, whose sense no more can feel
But his own wringing! What infinite heart's ease
Must kings neglect that private men enjoy!
And what have kings that privates have not too,
Save ceremony, save general ceremony?
And what art thou, thou idol ceremony?
What kind of god art thou, that suffer'st more
Of mortal griefs than do thy worshippers?
What are thy rents? What are thy comings-in?
O ceremony, show me but thy worth!
What is thy soul of adoration?
Art thou aught else but place, degree, and form,
Creating awe and fear in other men?
Wherein thou art less happy, being feared,
Than they in fearing.
What drink'st thou oft, instead of homage sweet,
But poisoned flattery? O, be sick, great greatness,
And bid thy ceremony give thee cure!
Thinks thou the fiery fever will go out
With titles blown from adulation?
Will it give place to flexure and low bending?

Canst thou, when thou command'st the beggar's knee,
Command the health of it? No, thou proud dream,
That play'st so subtly with a king's repose.
I am a king that find thee, and I know
'Tis not the balm, the sceptre, and the ball,
The sword, the mace, the crown imperial,
The intertissued robe of gold and pearl,
The farcèd tide running fore the king,
The throne he sits on, nor the tide of pomp
That beats upon the high shore of this world –
No, not all these, thrice-gorgeous ceremony,
Not all these, laid in bed majestical,
Can sleep so soundly as the wretched slave
Who, with a body filled and vacant mind,
Gets him to rest, crammed with distressful bread;
Never sees horrid night, the child of hell,
But, like a lackey, from the rise to set
Sweats in the eye of Phoebus, and all night
Sleeps in Elysium; next day after dawn,
Doth rise and help Hyperion to his horse;
And follows so the ever-running year
With profitable labour to his grave.
And but for ceremony, such a wretch,
Winding up days with toil, and nights with sleep,
Had the fore-hand and vantage of a king.
The slave, a member of the country's peace,
Enjoys it, but in gross brain little wots
What watch the king keeps to maintain the peace
Whose hours the peasant best advantages.

[IV, i, 282–98] *On the eve of the Battle of Agincourt, Harry knows if his men realise the odds are against them they will flee the battle, while if God measures Harry by the crimes of his father, He will strike him from his throne:*

O God of battles, steel my soldiers' hearts;
  Possess them not with fear; take from them now
The sense of reckoning, if th' opposèd numbers
Pluck their hearts from them. Not today, O Lord,
O, not today, think not upon the fault
My father made in compassing the crown!
I Richard's body have interrèd new,
And on it have bestowed more contrite tears
Than from it issued forcèd drops of blood.
Five hundred poor I have in yearly pay,
Who twice a day their withered hands hold up
Toward heaven, to pardon blood: and I have built
Two chantries where the sad and solemn priests
Sing still for Richard's soul. More will I do,
Though all that I can do is nothing worth,
Since that my penitence comes after all,
Imploring pardon.

JULIUS CAESAR

[II, i, 10–34] *Brutus is resolute, Caesar must die:*

It must be by his death; and, for my part,
I know no personal cause to spurn at him,
But for the general. – He would be crowned.
How that might change his nature, there's the question.
It is the bright day that brings forth the adder,
And that craves wary walking. Crown him! – that!
And then, I grant, we put a sting in him
That at his will he may do danger with.
Th'abuse of greatness is when it disjoins
Remorse from power; and, to speak truth of Caesar,
I have not known when his affections swayed
More than his reason. But 'tis a common proof
That lowliness is young ambition's ladder,
Whereto the climber-upward turns his face;
But when he once attains the upmost round,
He then unto the ladder turns his back,
Looks in the clouds, scorning the base degrees
By which he did ascend: so Caesar may;
Then, lest he may, prevent. And, since the quarrel
Will bear no colour for the thing he is,
Fashion it thus: that what he is, augmented,
Would run to these and these extremities;
And therefore think him as a serpent's egg
Which, hatched, would as his kind grow mischievous,
And kill him in the shell.

[II, i, 61–9] *Brutus blames Cassius' whisperings for his growing unease:*

Since Cassius first did whet me against Caesar
I have not slept.
Between the acting of a dreadful thing
And the first motion, all the interim is
Like a phantasma or a hideous dream:
The genius and the mortal instruments
Are then in council; and the state of man,
Like to a little kingdom, suffers then
The nature of an insurrection.

[II, i, 77–85] *As his unease grows, Brutus wonders why, if their cause is just, is there such need for secrecy?*

O conspiracy,
Sham'st thou to show thy dangerous brow
by night,
When evils are most free? O then, by day
Where wilt thou find a cavern dark enough
To mask thy monstrous visage? Seek none, conspiracy;
Hide it in smiles and affability;
For if thou path, thy native semblance on,
Not Erebus itself were dim enough
To hide thee from prevention.

[III, i, 254–75] *Mark Antony speaks over the body of his slain friend Caesar:*

O, pardon me, thou bleeding piece of earth,
That I am meek and gentle with these butchers!
Thou art the ruins of the noblest man
That ever livèd in the tide of times.
Woe to the hand that shed his costly blood!
Over thy wounds now do I prophesy –
Which like dumb mouths do ope their ruby lips
To beg the voice and utterance of my tongue –
A curse shall light upon the limbs of men;
Domestic fury and fierce civil strife
Shall cumber all the parts of Italy;
Blood and destruction shall be so in use,
And dreadful objects so familiar,
That mothers shall but smile when they behold
Their infants quartered with the hands of war,
All pity choked with custom of fell deeds;
And Caesar's spirit, ranging for revenge,
With Ate by his side come hot from hell,
Shall in these confines with a monarch's voice
Cry havoc and let slip the dogs of war,
That this foul deed shall smell above the earth
With carrion men, groaning for burial.

[III, ii, 1–10] *Inspired by love, Orlando sets to carve every tree in the forest with his beloved's name:*

H ang there, my verse, in witness of my love,
 And thou, thrice crownèd queen of night, survey
With thy chaste eye, from thy pale sphere above,
Thy huntress' name that my full life doth sway.
O Rosalind, these trees shall be my books
And in their barks my thoughts I'll character
That every eye which in this forest looks
Shall see thy virtue witnessed everywhere.
Run, run, Orlando; carve on every tree
The fair, the chaste, and unexpressive she.

HAMLET

[I, ii, 129–59] Hamlet seethes at what he sees as a futile future full of disappointment in a world 'weary, stale flat and unprofitable'. A world in which his father has been murdered and his mother remarried in less than two months.

O that this too too sullied flesh would melt,
Thaw, and resolve itself into a dew;
Or that the Everlasting had not fixed
His canon 'gainst self-slaughter. O God, God,
How weary, stale, flat, and unprofitable
Seem to me all the uses of this world!
Fie on't! ah, fie, 'tis an unweeded garden
That grows to seed. Things rank and gross in nature
Possess it merely. That it should come to this –
But two months dead, nay, not so much, not two!
So excellent a king, that was to this
Hyperion to a satyr; so loving to my mother
That he might not beteem the winds of heaven
Visit her face too roughly. Heaven and earth,
Must I remember? Why, she would hang on him
As if increase of appetite had grown
By what it fed on. And yet, within a month –
Let me not think on't. Frailty, thy name is woman.
A little month, or e'er those shoes were old
With which she followed my poor father's body
Like Niobe, all tears, why she, even she –
O God! A beast that wants discourse of reason
Would have mourned longer – married with my uncle,
My father's brother, but no more like my father

Than I to Hercules. Within a month,
Ere yet the salt of most unrighteous tears
Had left the flushing in her gallèd eyes,
She married. O, most wicked speed, to post
With such dexterity to incestuous sheets!
It is not, nor it cannot come to good.
But break, my heart, for I must hold my tongue.

[I, v, 92–112] *Hamlet vows never to forget:*

O all you host of heaven! O earth! What else?
And shall I couple hell? O, fie! Hold, hold, my
    heart.
And you, my sinews, grow not instant old,
But bear me stiffly up. Remember thee?
Ay, thou poor ghost, while memory holds a seat
In this distracted globe. Remember thee?
Yea, from the table of my memory
I'll wipe away all trivial fond records,
All saws of books, all forms, all pressures past
That youth and observation copied there,
And thy commandment all alone shall live
Within the book and volume of my brain,
Unmixed with baser matter. Yes, by heaven!
O most pernicious woman!
O villain, villain, smiling, damnèd villain!
My tables – meet it is I set it down
That one may smile, and smile, and be a villain.
At least I am sure it may be so in Denmark.
        (*He writes*)
So, uncle, there you are. Now to my word:

It is 'Adieu, adieu, remember me'.
I have sworn't.

[II, ii, 547–603] *As Hamlet reveals his plot to catch the king
in his guilt, he also exposes his true conflict — he is committed
to seeking revenge for his father, yet his revulsion toward
extracting a cold and calculating revenge renders him unable
to act:*

O what a rogue and peasant slave am I!
 Is it not monstrous that this player here,
But in a fiction, in a dream of passion,
Could force his soul so to his own conceit
That, from her working, all his visage wanned,
Tears in his eyes, distraction in his aspect,
A broken voice, and his whole function suiting
With forms to his conceit? And all for nothing.
For Hecuba!
What's Hecuba to him, or he to Hecuba,
That he should weep for her? What would he do
Had he the motive and the cue for passion
That I have? He would drown the stage with tears
And cleave the general ear with horrid speech,
Make mad the guilty and appal the free,
Confound the ignorant, and amaze indeed
The very faculties of eyes and ears. Yet I,
A dull and muddy-mettled rascal, peak
Like John-a-dreams, unpregnant of my cause,
And can say nothing, no, not for a king
Upon whose property and most dear life
A damned defeat was made. Am I a coward?

Who calls me villain? Breaks my pate across?
Plucks off my beard and blows it in my face?
Tweaks me by the nose? Gives me the lie i'th' throat
As deep as to the lungs? Who does me this?
Ha, 'swounds, I should take it. For it cannot be
But I am pigeon-livered and lack gall
To make oppression bitter, or ere this
I should ha' fatted all the region kites
With this slave's offal. Bloody bawdy villain!
Remorseless, treacherous, lecherous, kindles villain!
O, vengeance!
Why, what an ass am I! This is most brave,
That I, the son of a dear father murdered,
Prompted to my revenge by heaven and hell,
Must like a whore unpack my heart with words
And fall a-cursing like a very drab,
A stallion! Fie upon't, foh!
About, my brain! Hum – I have heard
That guilty creatures sitting at a play
Have by the very cunning of the scene
Been struck so to the soul that presently
They have proclaimed their malefactions.
For murder, though it have no tongue, will speak
With most miraculous organ, I'll have these players
Play something like the murder of my father
Before mine uncle. I'll observe his looks.
I'll tent him to the quick. If he do blench,
I know my course. The spirit that I have seen
May be a devil, and the devil hath power
T' assume a pleasing shape, yea, and perhaps
Out of my weakness and my melancholy,

As he is very potent with such spirits,
Abuses me to damn me. I'll have grounds
More relative than this. The play's the thing
Wherein I'll catch the conscience of the King.

[III, i, 56–88] *Hamlet contemplates suicide:*

To be, or not to be – that is the question;
   Whether 'tis nobler in the mind to suffer
The slings and arrows of outrageous fortune
Or to take arms against a sea of troubles
And by opposing end them. To die, to sleep –
No more – and by a sleep to say we end
The heartache, and the thousand natural shocks
That flesh is heir to. 'Tis a consummation
Devoutly to be wished. To die – to sleep –
To sleep – perchance to dream. Ay, there's the rub.
For in that sleep of death what dreams may come
When we have shuffled off this mortal coil
Must give us pause. There's the respect
That makes calamity of so long life.
For who would bear the whips and scorns of time,
Th' oppressor's wrong, the proud man's contumely,
The pangs of despised love, the law's delay,
The insolence of office, and the spurns
That patient merit of th' unworthy takes,
When he himself might his quietus make
With a bare bodkin? Who would these fardels bear,
To grunt and sweat under a weary life,
But that the dread of something after death,
The undiscovered country, from whose bourn

No traveller returns, puzzles the will,
And makes us rather bear those ills we have
Than fly to others that we know not of?
Thus conscience does make cowards of us all;
And thus the native hue of resolution
Is sicklied o'er with the pale cast of thought,
And enterprises of great pith and moment
With this regard their currents turn awry
And lose the name of action.

[III, ii, 395–406] *Hamlet tries to steel himself for action by preparing to challenge his mother with the wrongs she has perpetrated against his father's memory:*

'Tis now the very witching time of night,
　When churchyards yawn, and hell itself
　　breathes out
Contagion to this world. Now could I drink hot blood
And do such bitter business as the day
Would quake to look on. Soft! now to my mother.
O heart, lose not thy nature; let not ever
The soul of Nero enter this firm bosom.
Let me be cruel, not unnatural.
I will speak daggers to her, but use none.
My tongue and soul in this be hypocrites.
How in my words somever she be shent,
To give them seals never, my soul, consent.

[III, iii, 36–72] *While at prayer, King Claudius acknowledges his monstrous crime but also concedes that he cannot find it in himself to repent:*

O, my offence is rank. It smells to heaven.
It hath the primal eldest curse upon't,
A brother's murder! Pray can I not,
Though inclination be as sharp as will.
My stronger guilt defeats my strong intent,
And like a man to double business bound
I stand in pause where I shall first begin,
And both neglect. What if this cursèd hand
Were thicker than itself with brother's blood,
Is there not rain enough in the sweet heavens
To wash it white as snow? Whereto serves mercy
But to confront the visage of offence?
And what's in prayer but this twofold force,
To be forestallèd ere we come to fall
Or pardoned being down? Then I'll look up.
My fault is past. But, O, what form of prayer
Can serve my turn? 'Forgive me my foul murder'?
That cannot be, since I am still possessed
Of those effects for which I did the murder,
My crown, mine own ambition, and my queen.
May one be pardoned and retain th' offence?
In the corrupted currents of this world
Offence's gilded hand may shove by justice;
And oft 'tis seen the wicked prize itself
Buys out the law; but 'tis not so above.
There is no shuffling. There the action lies
In his true nature, and we ourselves compelled,

Even to the teeth and forehead of our faults,
To give in evidence. What then? What rests?
Try what repentance can. What can it not?
Yet what can it when one cannot repent?
O, wretched state! O, bosom black as death!
O limèd soul, that, struggling to be free
Art more engaged! Help, angels! Make assay.
Bow, stubborn knees, and heart with strings of steel,
Be soft as sinews of the new-born babe.
All may be well.

[III, iii, 73–95] *Hamlet discovers Claudius at prayer, and sees an opportunity to exact his revenge, but hesitates, fearing if he kills him now, he may send to heaven as soul that should be damned to hell:*

Now might I do it pat, now 'a is a-praying.
    And now I'll do't. And so 'a goes to heaven.
And so am I revenged. That would be scanned.
A villain kills my father, and for that,
I, his sole son, do this same villain send
To heaven.
Why, this is hire and salary, not revenge.
'A took my father grossly, full of bread,
With all his crimes broad blown, as flush as May;
And how his audit stands, who knows save heaven?
But in our circumstance and course of thought,
'Tis heavy with him! And am I then revenged,
To take him in the purging of his soul,
When he is fit and seasoned for his passage?
No.

Up, sword, and know thou a more horrid hent.
When he is drunk asleep; or in his rage,
Or in th'incestuous pleasure of his bed,
At game, a-swearing, or about some act
That has no relish of salvation in't –
Then trip him, that his heels may kick at heaven,
And that his soul may be as damned and black
As hell, whereto it goes.

[IV, iv, 32–66] *Hearing of a war that is to be fought over a small piece of land, Hamlet has cause to reflect on his failure to avenge the most atrocious of crimes:*

How all occasions do inform against me
And spur my dull revenge! What is a man,
If his chief good and market of his time
Be but to sleep and feed? A beast, no more.
Sure He that made us with such large discourse,
Looking before and after, gave us not
That capability and godlike reason
To fust in us unused. Now, whether it be
Bestial oblivion, or some craven scruple
Of thinking too precisely on th' event –
A thought which, quartered, hath but one part wisdom
And ever three parts coward – I do not know
Why yet I live to say 'This thing's to do',
Sith I have cause, and will, and strength, and means
To do't. Examples gross as earth exhort me.
Witness this army of such mass and charge,
Led by a delicate and tender prince,
Whose spirit, with divine ambition puffed,

Makes mouths at the invisible event,
Exposing what is mortal and unsure
To all that fortune, death, and danger dare,
Even for an eggshell. Rightly to be great
Is not to stir without great argument,
But greatly to find quarrel in a straw
When honour's at the stake. How stand I then,
That have a father killed, a mother stained,
Excitements of my reason and my blood,
And let all sleep, while to my shame I see
The imminent death of twenty thousand men
That for a fantasy and trick of fame
Go to their graves like beds, fight for a plot
Whereon the numbers cannot try the cause,
Which is not tomb enough and continent
To hide the slain? O, from this time forth,
My thoughts be bloody, or be nothing worth!

[II, ii, 17–41] *When the beautiful Olivia is duped by Viola's disguise and sends her a love token Viola has cause to consider the influence of the male form on female sense:*

I left no ring with her; what means this lady?
Fortune forbid my outside have not charmed her!
She made good view of me; indeed, so much
That – methought – her eyes had lost her tongue,
For she did speak in starts, distractedly.
She loves me, sure, the cunning of her passion
Invites me in this churlish messenger.
None of my lord's ring! Why, he sent her none.
I am the man! If it be so – as 'tis –
Poor lady, she were better love a dream.
Disguise, I see thou art a wickedness
Wherein the pregnant enemy does much.
How easy is it for the proper false
In women's waxen hearts to set their forms.
Alas, our frailty is the cause, not we,
For such as we are made of, such we be.
How will this fadge? My master loves her dearly;
And I, poor monster, fond as much on him;
And she, mistaken, seems to dote on me.
What will become of this? As I am man,
My state is desperate for my master's love.
As I am woman – now alas the day,
What thriftless sighs shall poor Olivia breathe!
O time, thou must untangle this, not I!
It is too hard a knot for me t' untie.

TROILUS AND CRESSIDA

[I, i, 91–106] *Prince Troilus is obsessed with his love affair with Cressida, the fact that his city is at war can not draw his attention from his agent in love, Lord Pandarus:*

Peace, you ungracious clamours! Peace, rude sounds!
Fools on both sides! Helen must needs be fair,
When with your blood you daily paint her thus.
I cannot fight upon this argument;
It is too starved a subject for my sword.
But Pandarus – O gods, how do you plague me!
I cannot come to Cressid but by Pandar,
And he's as tetchy to be wooed to woo
As she is stubborn-chaste against all suit.
Tell me, Apollo, for thy Daphne's love,
What Cressid is, what Pandar, and what we –
Her bed is India; there she lies, a pearl:
Between our Ilium and where she resides,
Let it be called the wild and wandering flood,
Ourself the merchant, and this sailing Pandar
Our doubtful hope, our convoy, and our bark.

[I, ii, 281–95] *Cressida is also conducting her love affair through and intermediary, although she finds this difficult, she knows enough to stand her ground on the battlefield of love:*

Words, vows, gifts, tears, and love's full sacrifice
He offers in another's enterprise;
But more in Troilus thousandfold I see

Than in the glass of Pandar's praise may be.
Yet hold I off. Women are angels, wooing;
Things won are done; joy's soul lies in the doing.
That she beloved knows naught that knows not this:
Men prize the thing ungained more than it is.
That she was never yet that ever knew
Love got so sweet as when desire did sue;
Therefore this maxim out of love I teach:
'Achievement is command; ungained, beseech.'
Then, though my heart's content firm love doth bear,
Nothing of that shall from mine eyes appear.

[III, ii, 16–27] *Enfeebled by the anticipation of Love, Troilus fears the reality of Love's pleasures may destroy him as effectively as the battlefield:*

I am giddy; expectation whirls me round.
Th' imaginary relish is so sweet
That it enchants my sense. What will it be,
When that watery palate tastes indeed
Love's thrice-repurèd nectar? – death, I fear me,
Swooning destruction, or some joy too fine,
Too subtle-potent, tuned too sharp in sweetness,
For the capacity of my ruder powers.
I fear it much; and I do fear besides
That I shall lose distinction in my joys,
As doth a battle, when they charge on heaps
The enemy flying.

SIR THOMAS MORE

[Addition III] Sir Thomas More, Lord Chancellor of England, recollects his meteoric rise to power and questions the price of fortune's gifts:

It is in heaven that I am thus and thus,
And that which we profanely term our fortunes
Is the provision of the power above,
Fitted and shaped just to that strength of nature
Which we are born withal. Good God! Good God!
That I from such an humble bench of birth
Should step as 'twere up to my country's head
And give the law out there – ay, in my father's life
To take prerogative and tithe of knees
From elder kinsmen, and him bind by my place
To give the smooth and dexter way to me
That owe it him by nature. Sure, these things
Not physicked by respect, might turn our blood
To much corruption. But More, the more thou hast –
Either of honour, office, wealth and calling,
Which might excite thee to embrace and hug them –
The more do thou in serpents' natures think them,
Fear their gay skins with thought of their sharp state
And let this be thy maxim: to be great
Is, when the thread of hazard is once spun,
A bottom great wound up, greatly undone.

[II, ii, 162–87] Despite resisting all previous feminine temptation, the pious Angelo cannot overcome his attraction to Isabella:

What's this? What's this? Is this her fault or
        mine?
The tempter or the tempted, who sins most?
Ha?
Not she, nor doth she tempt; but it is I
That, lying by the violet in the sun,
Do as the carrion does, not as the flower,
Corrupt with virtuous season. Can it be
That modesty may more betray our sense
Than woman's lightness? Having waste ground
        enough,
Shall we desire to raze the sanctuary,
And pitch our evils there? O, fie, fie, fie!
What dost thou? Or what art thou, Angelo?
Dost thou desire her foully for those things
That make her good? O, let her brother live:
Thieves for their robbery have authority
When judges steal themselves. What, do I love her,
That I desire to hear her speak again,
And feast upon her eyes? What is't I dream on?
O cunning enemy, that, to catch a saint,
With saints dost bait thy hook. Most dangerous
Is that temptation that doth goad us on
To sin in loving virtue. Never could the strumpet,
With all her double vigour, art and nature,

Once stir my temper; but this virtuous maid
Subdues me quite. Ever till now,
When men were fond, I smiled and wondered how.

[II, iv, 1–17] *Angelo fears for his faith as he battles his unholy
attraction to Isabella:*

When I would pray and think, I think and pray
　　To several subjects: heaven hath my empty
　　　　words,
Whilst my invention, hearing not my tongue,
Anchors on Isabel: God in my mouth,
As if I did but only chew His name,
And in my heart the strong and swelling evil
Of my conception. The state, whereon I studied,
Is like a good thing being often read,
Grown seared and tedious; yea, my gravity,
Wherein, let no man hear me, I take pride,
Could I with boot change for an idle plume
Which the air beats for vain. O place, O form,
How often dost thou with thy case, thy habit,
Wrench awe from fools, and tie the wiser souls
To thy false seeming! Blood, thou art blood;
Let's write 'good Angel' on the devil's horn;
'Tis not the devil's crest.

[III, i, 517–38] *The Duke of Vienna is livid at what he sees
as Angelo's hypocrisy. The Duke decides to create a deception
with which to counter Angelo's behaviour. Angelo has convinced
Isabella to sleep with him to save her brother's life; but the
Duke will arrange for Antonio's spurned lover, Mariana, to go
in Isabella's place:*

He who the sword of heaven will bear
Should be as holy as severe;
Pattern in himself to know,
Grace to stand, and virtue go;
More nor less to others paying
Than by self-offences weighing.
Shame to him whose cruel striking
Kills for faults of his own liking.
Twice treble shame on Angelo,
To weed my vice and let his grow.
O, what may man within him hide,
Though angel on the outward side?
How may likeness made in crimes,
Make a practice on the times,
To draw with idle spiders' strings
Most ponderous and substantial things!
Craft against vice I must apply.
With Angelo tonight shall lie
His old betrothed but despised:
So disguise shall by th' disguised
Pay with falsehood false exacting,
And perform an old contracting.

OTHELLO

[III, iii, 225–74] *The tragic Othello lets his own jealousy
and Iago's lies convince him that his beloved Desdemona is his
betrayer:*

This fellow's of exceeding honesty,
    And knows all qualities, with a learnèd spirit
Of human dealings. If I do prove her haggard,
Though that her jesses were my dear heart-strings,
I'd whistle her off and let her down the wind
To prey at fortune. Haply, for I am black
And have not those soft parts of conversation
That chamberers have; or for I am declined
Into the vale of years – yet that's not much –
She's gone: I am abused, and my relief
Must be to loathe her. O, curse of marriage!
That we can call these delicate creatures ours
And not their appetites! I had rather be a toad
And live upon the vapour of a dungeon,
Than keep a corner in the thing I love
For others' uses. Yet, 'tis the plague of great ones;
Prerogatived are they less than the base.
'Tis destiny unshunnable, like death:
Even then this forked plague is fated to us
When we do quicken:

[V, ii, 1–22] *His frantic jealousy has convinced Othello of his wife's infidelity, and he resolves to murder Desdemona:*

It is the cause, it is the cause, my soul:
Let me not name it to you, you chaste stars!
It is the cause. Yet I'll not shed her blood,
Nor scar that whiter skin of hers than snow,
And smooth as monumental alabaster:
Yet she must die, else she'll betray more men.
Put out the light, and then put out the light:
If I quench thee, thou flaming minister,
I can again thy former light restore,
Should I repent me; but once put out thy light,
Thou cunning'st pattern of excelling nature,
I know not where is that Promethean heat
That can thy light relume. When I have plucked thy
    rose,
I cannot give it vital growth again,
It must needs wither. I'll smell it on the tree.
    He kisses her
O, balmy breath, that dost almost persuade
Justice to break her sword! One more, one more.
Be thus when thou art dead and I will kill thee,
And love thee after. One more, and this the last.
So sweet was ne'er so fatal. I must weep.
But they are cruel tears; this sorrow's heavenly –
It strikes where it doth love. She wakes.

[I, i, 78–97] *Helena knows she should mourn for her recently dead father, but she finds these emotions are overtaken by her love for Bertram:*

O, were that all! I think not on my father,
    And these great tears grace his remembrance
       more
Than those I shed for him. What was he like?
I have forgot him; my imagination
Carries no favour in't but Bertram's.
I am undone: there is no living, none,
If Bertram be away. 'Twere all one
That I should love a bright particular star
And think to we'd it, he is so above me.
In his bright radiance and collateral light
Must I be comforted, not in his sphere.
Th' ambition in my love thus plagues itself:
The hind that would be mated by the lion
Must die for love. 'Twas pretty, though a plague,
To see him every hour; to sit and draw
His archèd brows, his hawking eye, his curls,
In our heart's table – heart too capable
Of every line and trick of his sweet favour.
But now he's gone, and my idolatrous fancy
Must sanctify his relics.

[IV, i, 1–41] Timon seeks refuge from the world of men in a wood outside the city. He is exhausted by generosity and has spent all of his money entertaining friends:

L et me look back upon thee. O thou wall
     That girdles in those wolves, dive in the earth
And fence not Athens. Matrons, turn incontinent.
Obedience, fail in children. Slaves and fools
Pluck the grave wrinkled Senate from the bench,
And minister in their steads. To general filths
Convert, o'th'instant, green virginity.
Do't in your parents' eyes. Bankrupts, hold fast;
Rather than render back, out with your knives
And cut your trusters' throats. Bound servants, steal.
Large-handed robbers your grave masters are,
And pill by law. Maid, to thy master's bed;
Thy mistress is o'th'brothel. Son of sixteen,
Pluck the lined crutch from thy old limping sire,
With it beat out his brains. Piety and fear,
Religion to the gods, peace, justice, truth,
Domestic awe, night-rest, and neighbourhood,
Instruction, manners, mysteries, and trades,
Degrees, observances, customs, and laws,
Decline to your confounding contraries
And let confusion live. Plagues incident to men,
Your potent and infectious fevers heap
On Athens, ripe for stroke. Thou cold sciatica,
Cripple our senators, that their limbs may halt
As lamely as their manners. Lust and liberty

Creep in the minds and marrows of our youth,
That 'gainst the stream of virtue they may strive,
And drown themselves in riot. Itches, blains,
Sow all th' Athenian bosoms, and their crop
Be general leprosy. Breath infect breath,
That their society, as their friendship, may
Be merely poison. Nothing I'll bear from thee
But nakedness, thou detestable town.
Take thou that too, with multiplying bans.
Timon will to the woods, where he shall find
Th' unkindest beast more kinder than mankind.
The gods confound – hear me, you good gods all –
The Athenians both within and out that wall.
And grant, as Timon grows, his hate may grow
To the whole race of mankind, high and low!
Amen.

[IV, iii, 1–45] *Timon broods that man's status in the world is
determined by wealth not worth. When he discovers gold, while
digging for roots, he is filled with satirical scorn for the 'damned
earth', 'the common whore of mankind':*

O blessed breeding sun, draw from the earth
Rotten humidity. Below thy sister's orb
Infect the air! Twinn'd brothers of one womb,
Whose procreation, residence, and birth,
Scarce is dividant – touch them with several fortunes,
The greater scorns the lesser. Not nature,
To whom all sores lay siege, can bear great fortune
But by contempt of nature.
Raise me this beggar and deject that lord –

The senator shall bear contempt hereditary,
The beggar native honour.
It is the pasture lards the wether's sides,
The want that makes him lean. Who dares, who dares,
In purity of manhood stand upright,
And say 'This man's a flatterer'? If one be,
So are they all, for every grise of fortune
Is smoothed by that below. The learnèd pate
Ducks to the golden fool. All's obliquy,
There's nothing level in our cursèd natures
But direct villainy. Therefore be abhorred
All feasts, societies, and throngs of men.
His semblable, yea, himself. Timon disdains.
Destruction fang mankind. Earth, yield me roots.
    He digs
Who seeks for better of thee, sauce his palate
With thy most operant poison. What is here?
Gold? Yellow, glittering, precious gold?
No, gods, I am no idle votarist.
Roots, you clear heavens! Thus much of this will make
Black white, foul fair, wrong right,
Base noble, old young, coward valiant.
Ha, you gods! Why this? What, this, you gods? Why,
    this
Will lug your priests and servants from your sides,
Pluck stout men's pillows from below their heads.
This yellow slave
Will knit and break religions, bless th' accursed,
Make the hoar leprosy adored, place thieves
And give them title, knee, and approbation,
With senators on the bench. This is it

That makes the wappened widow wed again –
She whom the spital-house and ulcerous sores
Would cast the gorge at, this embalms and spices
To th'April day again. Come, damned earth,
Thou common whore of mankind, that puts odds
Among the rout of nations, I will make thee
Do thy right nature.

[I, ii, 1–22] *Glouster's bastard son, Edmund, decides he is no less worthy than his legitimate brother:*

Thou, Nature, art my goddess; to thy law
  My services are bound. Wherefore should I
Stand in the plague of custom and permit
The curiosity of nations to deprive me,
For that I am some twelve or fourteen moonshines
Lag of a brother? Why bastard? Wherefore base?
When my dimensions are as well-compact,
My mind as generous, and my shape as true
As honest madam's issue? Why brand they us
With 'base'? with 'baseness'? 'bastardy'? 'base, base'?
Who in the lusty stealth of nature take
More composition and fierce quality
Than doth, within a dull, stale, tired bed
Go to the creating a whole tribe of fops
Got 'tween asleep and wake? Well then,
Legitimate Edgar, I must have your land.
Our father's love is to the bastard Edmund
As to the legitimate. Fine word 'legitimate'!
Well, my 'legitimate', if this letter speed
And my invention thrive, Edmund the base
Shall top the legitimate. I grow. I prosper.
Now, gods stand up for bastards!

[II, iii, 1–21] *Edgar's situation is so desperate — his father turned against him by his bastard brother's machinations — that as he flees for his life he can see no more apt disguise than that of a ranting Bedlam beggar:*

I heard myself proclaimed,
  And by the happy hollow of a tree
Escaped the hunt. No port is free, no place
That guard and most unusual vigilance
Does not attend my taking. Whiles I may 'scape
I will preserve myself; and am bethought
To take the basest and most poorest shape
That ever penury, in contempt of man,
Brought near to beast. My face I'll grime with filth,
Blanket my loins, elf all my hair in knots,
And with presented nakedness outface
The winds and persecutions of the sky,
The country gives me proof and precedent
Of Bedlam beggars, who, with roaring voices,
Strike in their numbed and mortified bare arms
Pins, wooden pricks, nails, sprigs of rosemary;
And with this horrible object, from low farms,
Poor pelting villages, sheepcotes, and mills
Sometime with lunatic bans, sometime with prayers,
Enforce their charity: 'Poor Turlygod! Poor Tom!'
That's something yet; Edgar I nothing am.

[IV, i, 1—9] *Still disguised as a Bedlam beggar, Edgar finds comfort in his position at the bottom of the social heap:*

Yet better thus, and known to be contemned
    Than still contemned and flattered. To be worst,
The lowest and most dejected thing of fortune,
Stands still in esperance, lives not in fear.
The lamentable change is from the best;
The worst returns to laughter. Welcome then,
Thou unsubstantial air that I embrace!
The wretch that thou hast blown unto the worst
Owes nothing to thy blasts.

[III, iv, 28—36] *His own lowly situation causes Lear to contemplate the lot of his country's poor:*

Poor naked wretches, wheresoe'er you are,
    That bide the pelting of this pitiless storm,
How shall your houseless heads and unfed sides,
Your looped and windowed raggedness, defend you
From seasons such as these? O, I have ta'en
Too little care of this! Take physic, pomp;
Expose thyself to feel what wretches feel,
That thou mayst shake the superflux to them
And show the heavens more just.

[I, v, 36–52] *Lady Macbeth realises a single murder stands between her husband and the Scottish throne and King Duncan is to be guest of honour this very night:*

The raven himself is hoarse
That croaks the fatal entrance of Duncan
Under my battlements. Come, you spirits
That tend on mortal thoughts, unsex me here
And fill me from the crown to the toe top-full
Of direst cruelty. Make thick my blood;
Stop up the access and passage to remorse,
That no compunctious visitings of nature
Shake my fell purpose nor keep peace between
The effect and it. Come to my woman's breasts
And take my milk for gall, you murdering ministers,
Wherever, in your sightless substances,
You wait on nature's mischief. Come, thick night,
And pall thee in the dunnest smoke of hell,
That my keen knife see not the wound it makes,
Nor heaven peep through the blanket of the dark
To cry, 'Hold, hold!'

[I, vii, 1–28] *Macbeth is appalled by the enormity of his wife's suggestion that Duncan should be murdered:*

If it were done when 'tis done, then 'twere well
It were done quickly. If the assassination
Could trammel up the consequence, and catch,
With his surcease, success – that but this blow

Might be the be-all and the end-all! – here,
But here, upon this bank and shoal of time,
We'd jump the life to come. But in these cases
We still have judgement here – that we but teach
Bloody instructions, which being taught return
To plague the inventor. This even-handed justice
Commends the ingredients of our poisoned chalice
To our own lips. He's here in double trust:
First, as I am his kinsman and his subject,
Strong both against the deed; then, as his host,
Who should against his murderer shut the door,
Not bear the knife myself. Besides, this Duncan
Hath borne his faculties so meek, hath been
So clear in his great office, that his virtues
Will plead like angels, trumpet-tongued against
The deep damnation of his taking-off;
And pity, like a naked new-born babe
Striding the blast, or heaven's cherubin, horsed
Upon the sightless curriers of the air,
Shall blow the horrid deed in every eye,
That tears shall drown the wind. I have no spur
To prick the sides of my intent, but only
Vaulting ambition, which o'erleaps itself
And falls on the other.

[II, i, 33–64] *As he gathers courage to murder the sleeping*
Duncan, Macbeth can no longer distinguish between his
fantasies of power and the reality of murder:

I s this a dagger which I see before me,
The handle toward my hand? Come, let me clutch thee –

I have thee not, and yet I see thee still!
Art thou not, fatal vision, sensible
To feeling as to sight? Or art thou but
A dagger of the mind, a false creation,
Proceeding from the heat-oppressèd brain?
I see thee yet, in form as palpable
As this which now I draw.
Thou marshall'st me the way that I was going,
And such an instrument I was to use. –
Mine eyes are made the fools o' the other senses,
Or else worth all the rest. – I see thee still,
And on thy blade and dudgeon, gouts of blood,
Which was not so before. There's no such thing:
It is the bloody business which informs
Thus to mine eyes. Now o'er the one half-world
Nature seems dead, and wicked dreams abuse
The curtained sleep. Witchcraft celebrates
Pale Hecat's offerings; and withered Murder,
Alarumed by his sentinel the wolf,
Whose howl's his watch, thus with his stealthy pace,
With Tarquin's ravishing strides, towards his design
Moves like a ghost. Thou sure and firm-set earth,
Hear not my steps, which way they walk, for fear
Thy very stones prate of my whereabout
And take the present horror from the time
Which now suits with it. – Whiles I threat, he lives:
Words to the heat of deeds too cold breath gives.
　　　(*A bell rings.*)
I go, and it is done; the bell invites me.
Hear it not, Duncan, for it is a knell
That summons thee to heaven, or to hell.

[V, v, 17–28] *On hearing of his wife's death, Macbeth withdraws into himself to contemplate the futility of his murderous actions:*

She should have died hereafter;
There would have been a time for such a word –
Tomorrow, and tomorrow, and tomorrow,
Creeps in this petty pace from day to day
To the last syllable of recorded time;
And all our yesterdays have lighted fools
The way to dusty death. Out, out, brief candle!
Life's but a walking shadow, a poor player
That struts and frets his hour upon the stage
And then is heard no more. It is a tale
Told by an idiot, full of sound and fury,
Signifying nothing.

[IV, xiv, 44–54] *Having parted from his lover, Cleopatra, on bad terms, Antony is devastated by the news of her death (she is in fact alive). He resolves to commit suicide so they can be reconciled in the afterlife:*

I will o'ertake thee, Cleopatra, and
Weep for my pardon. So it must be, for now
All length is torture; since the torch is out,
Lie down, and stray no farther. Now all labour
Mars what it does; yea, very force entangles
Itself with strength. Seal then, and all is done.
Eros! – I come, my queen – Eros! Stay for me.
Where souls do couch on flowers, we'll hand in hand,
And with our sprightly port make the ghosts gaze:
Dido and her Aeneas shall want troops,
And all the haunt be ours.

[I, i, 122–43] *Pericles is appalled when he understands that his intended bride has been the incestuous lover of her father, King Antiochus:*

How courtesy would seem to cover sin,
   When what is done is like an hypocrite,
The which is good in nothing but in sight.
If it be true that I interpret false,
Then were it certain you were not so bad
As with foul incest to abuse your soul;
Where now you're both a father and a son
By your untimely claspings with your child,
Which pleasures fits a husband, not a father,
And she, an eater of her mother's flesh
By the defiling of her parents' bed;
And both like serpents are, who though they feed
On sweetest flowers, yet they poison breed.
Antioch, farewell, for wisdom sees those men
Blush not in actions blacker than the night
Will shun no course to keep them from the light.
One sin, I know, another doth provoke.
Murder's as near to lust as flame to smoke.
Poison and treason are the hands of sin,
Ay, and the targets to put off the shame.
Then, lest my life be cropped to keep you clear,
By flight I'll shun the danger which I fear.

[II, i, 1–11] *Pericles rales against the storm that has destroyed his ship: it has proved its dominance, now he wishes it would leave him to die in peace:*

Yet cease your ire, you angry stars of heaven!
   Wind, rain, and thunder, remember earthly man
Is but a substance that must yield to you,
And I, as fits my nature, do obey you.
Alas, the seas hath cast me on the rocks,
Washed me from shore to shore, and left my breath
Nothing to think on but ensuing death.
Let it suffice the greatness of your powers
To have bereft a prince of all his fortunes,
And, having thrown him from your watery grave
Here to have death in peace is all he'll crave.

CORIOLANUS

[IV, iv, 12–26] *Coriolanus find himself exiled in the enemy city of Antium. He resolves to find his old adversary, Aufidius:*

O world, thy slippery turns! Friends now fast
    sworn,
Whose double bosoms seems to wear one heart,
Whose hours, whose bed, whose meal and exercise
Are still together, who twin, as 'twere, in love
Unseparable, shall within this hour,
On a dissension of a doit, break out
To bitterest enmity. So fellest foes,
Whose passions and whose plots have broke their sleep
To take the one the other, by some chance,
Some trick not worth an egg, shall grow dear friends
And interjoin their issues. So with me.
My birthplace hate I, and my love's upon
This enemy town. I'll enter. If he slay me,
He does fair justice: if he give me way,
I'll do his country service.

[III, iii, 58–76] *King Leontes believes his wife has been unfaithful and that their baby is in fact her bastard offspring. He orders the baby abandoned in the wilderness, fortunately the child is discovered by an elderly shepherd:*

I would there were no age between ten and three-and-twenty, or that youth would sleep out the rest: for there is nothing in the between but getting wenches with child, wronging the ancientry, stealing, fighting. Hark you now: would any but these boiled brains of nineteen and two-and-twenty hunt this weather? They have scared away two of my best sheep, which I fear the wolf will sooner find than the master. If anywhere I have them, 'tis by the sea-side, browsing of ivy. Good luck, an't be thy will!

He sees the child
What have we here? Mercy on's, a barne! A very pretty barne. A boy or a child, I wonder? A pretty one, a very pretty one. Sure, some scape. Though I am not bookish, yet I can read waiting gentlewoman in the scape: this has been some stair-work, some trunk-work, some behind-door-work. They were warmer that got this than the poor thing is here. I'll take it up for pity – yet I'll tarry till my son come: he hallowed but even now. Whoa-ho-hoa!

[II, ii, 12–51] *On hearing Giacomo brag that he can seduce*
any woman he wants, Posthumus has bet on the chastity of his
wife Imogen. Desperate to win the bet, Giacomo has hidden in
a trunk in Imogen's bed chamber so he can convince Posthumus
he has won the bet. Emerging from hiding, he begins to recall
details of Imogen's room and body: he may have left her body
untouched but he will destroy her reputation:

The crickets sing, and man's o'er-laboured sense
      Repairs itself by rest. Our Tarquin thus
Did softly press the rushes ere he waken'd
The chastity he wounded. Cytherea,
How bravely thou becom'st thy bed! Fresh lily,
And whiter than the sheets! That I might touch!
But kiss; one kiss! Rubies unparagoned,
How dearly they do 't! 'Tis her breathing that
Perfumes the chamber thus. The flame o' th' taper
Bows toward her and would under-peep her lids
To see th' enclosed lights, now canopied
Under these windows white and azure, lac'd
With blue of heaven's own tinct. But my design
To note the chamber. I will write all down:
Such and such pictures; there the window; such
Th' adornment of her bed; the arras, figures –
Why, such and such; and the contents o' th' story.
Ah, but some natural notes about her body
Above ten thousand meaner movables
Would testify, t' enrich mine inventory.
O sleep, thou ape of death, lie dull upon her!

And be her sense but as a monument,
Thus in a chapel lying! Come off, come off;
    (*Taking off her bracelet*)
As slippery as the Gordian knot was hard!
'Tis mine; and this will witness outwardly,
As strongly as the conscience does within,
To th' madding of her lord. On her left breast
A mole cinque-spotted, like the crimson drops
I' the' bottom of a cowslip. Here's a voucher
Stronger than ever law could make; this secret
Will force him think I have picked the lock and ta'en
The treasure of her honour. No more. To what end?
Why should I write this down that's riveted,
Screw'd to my memory? She hath been reading late
The tale of Tereus; here the leaf's turned down
Where Philomel gave up. I have enough.
To th' trunk again, and shut the spring of it.
Swift, swift, you dragons of the night, that dawning
May bare the raven's eye! I lodge in fear;
Though this a heavenly angel, hell is here.
    (*Clock strikes*)
One, two, three. Time, time!

[II, v, 1–35] *On hearing Giacomo's tale of conquest, Posthumus
is left feeling his life is in tatters, his faith destroyed:*

I s there no way for men to be, but women
  Must be half-workers? We are all bastards,
And that most venerable man which I
Did call my father was I know not where
When I was stamped. Some coiner with his tools

Made me a counterfeit; yet my mother seem'd
The Dian of that time. So doth my wife
The nonpareil of this. O, vengeance, vengeance!
Me of my lawful pleasure she restrained,
And prayed me oft forbearance; did it with
A pudency so rosy, the sweet view on't
Might well have warmed old Saturn; that I thought her
As chaste as unsunned snow. O, all the devils!
This yellow Iachimo in an hour – was't not?
Or less! – at first? Perchance he spoke not, but,
Like a full-acorned boar, a German one,
Cried 'O!' and mounted; found no opposition
But what he look'd for should oppose and she
Should from encounter guard. Could I find out
The woman's part in me! For there's no motion
That tends to vice in man but I affirm
It is the woman's part. Be it lying, note it,
The woman's; flattering, hers; deceiving, hers;
Lust and rank thoughts, hers, hers; revenges, hers;
Ambitions, covetings, change of prides, disdain,
Nice longing, slanders, mutability,
All faults that man may name, nay, that hell knows,
Why, hers, in part or all; but rather all;
For even to vice
They are not constant, but are changing still
One vice but of a minute old for one
Not half so old as that. I'll write against them,
Detest them, curse them. Yet 'tis greater skill
In a true hate to pray they have their will:
The very devils cannot plague them better.

[III, vi, 1–27] *Filled with joy at the prospect of meeting her husband, Imogen discovers his plot to seek revenge for her alleged adultery. Disguised in a man's clothing, she continues her journey, resolved to convince him of her fidelity:*

I see a man's life is a tedious one.
I have tir'd myself, and for two nights together
Have made the ground my bed. I should be sick
But that my resolution helps me. Milford,
When from the mountain-top Pisanio showed thee,
Thou wast within a ken. O Jove! I think
Foundations fly the wretched; such, I mean,
Where they should be relieved. Two beggars told me
I could not miss my way. Will poor folks lie,
That have afflictions on them, knowing 'tis
A punishment or trial? Yes; no wonder,
When rich ones scarce tell true. To lapse in fullness
Is sorer than to lie for need; and falsehood
Is worse in kings than beggars. My dear lord!
Thou art one o' th' false ones. Now I think on thee
My hunger's gone; but even before, I was
At point to sink for food. But what is this?
Here is a path to 't; 'tis some savage hold.
I were best not call; I dare not call. Yet famine,
Ere clean it o'erthrow nature, makes it valiant.
Plenty and peace breeds cowards; hardness ever
Of hardiness is mother. Ho! Who's here?
If anything that's civil, speak; if savage,
Take or lend. Ho! No answer? Then I'll enter.
Best draw my sword; and if mine enemy

But fear the sword, like me, he'll scarcely look on't.
Such a foe, good heavens!

[IV, ii, 293–334] *Almost mad with grief, as she continues her journey, Imogen wakes to find herself beside what appears to be the headless body of her husband:*

Yes, sir, to Milford Haven. Which is the way?
    I thank you. By yond bush? Pray, how far
        thither?
'Ods pittikins! Can it be six mile yet?
I have gone all night. Faith, I'll lie down and sleep.
But, soft! no bedfellow. O gods and goddesses!
    (*Seeing the body*)
These flow'rs are like the pleasures of the world;
This bloody man, the care on't. I hope I dream;
For so I thought I was a cave-keeper,
And cook to honest creatures. But 'tis not so;
'Twas but a bolt of nothing, shot at nothing,
Which the brain makes of fumes. Our very eyes
Are sometimes, like our judgements, blind. Good faith,
I tremble still with fear; but if there be
Yet left in heaven as small a drop of pity
As a wren's eye, feared gods, a part of it!
The dream's here still. Even when I wake it is
Without me, as within me; not imagined, felt.
A headless man? The garments of Posthumus?
I know the shape of his leg; this is his hand,
His foot mercurial, his martial thigh,
The brawns of Hercules; but his jovial face –
Murder in heaven! How!

[V, v, 97–123] *Imprisoned, Posthumus feels his fate is just*
payment for his treatment of Imogen:

Most welcome, bondage! For thou art a way,
I think, to liberty. Yet am I better
Than one that's sick o' th' gout, since he had rather
Groan so in perpetuity than be cured
By th' sure physician death, who is the key
T' unbar these locks. My conscience, thou art fettered
More than my shanks and wrists; you good gods, give me
The penitent instrument to pick that bolt,
Then, free for ever! Is't enough I am sorry?
So children temporal fathers do appease;
Gods are more full of mercy. Must I repent,
I cannot do it better than in gyves,
Desired more than constrained. To satisfy,
If of my freedom 'tis the main part, take
No stricter render of me than my all.
I know you are more clement than vile men,
Who of their broken debtors take a third,
A sixth, a tenth, letting them thrive again
On their abatement; that's not my desire.
For Imogen's dear life take mine; and though
'Tis not so dear, yet 'tis a life; you coined it.
'Tween man and man they weigh not every stamp;
Though light, take pieces for the figure's sake;
You rather mine, being yours. And so, great pow'rs,
If you will take this audit, take this life,
And cancel these cold bonds. O Imogen!
I'll speak to thee in silence.
     (*Sleeps*)

[II, ii, 1–17] *Caliban feels his right to rule the island has been usurped by Prospero:*

All the infections that the sun sucks up
    From bogs, fens, flats, on Prosper fall, and make him
By inch-meal a disease! His spirits hear me,
And yet I needs must curse. But they'll nor pinch,
Fright me with urchin-shows, pitch me i' th' mire,
Nor lead me, like a firebrand, in the dark
Out of my way, unless he bid 'em; but
For every trifle are they set upon me;
Sometime like apes that mow and chatter at me,
And after bite me; then like hedgehogs which
Lie tumbling in my barefoot way, and mount
Their pricks at my footfall. Sometime am I
All wound with adders, who with cloven tongues
Do hiss me into madness.
    Enter Trinculo
Lo, now, lo!
Here comes a spirit of his, and to torment me
For bringing wood in slowly. I'll fall flat.
Perchance he will not mind me.

[II, ii, 18–40] *Washed ashore by the storm, Trinculo ponders the sleeping Caliban:*

Here's neither bush nor shrub to bear off any
weather at all, and another storm brewing.
I hear it sing i' th' wind. Yond same black cloud, yond
huge one, looks like a foul bombard that would shed
his liquor. If it should thunder as it did before, I know
not where to hide my head. Yond same cloud cannot
choose but fall by pailfuls. What have we here?
A man or a fish? Dead or alive? A fish! He smells
like a fish; a very ancient and fish-like smell; kind of
not-of-the-newest poor-John. A strange fish! Were
I in England now, as once I was, and had but this fish
painted, not a holiday fool there but would give a piece
of silver. There would this monster make a man. Any
strange beast there makes a man. When they will not
give a doit to relieve a lame beggar, they will lay out
ten to see a dead Indian. Legged like a man! And his
fins like arms! Warm, o' my troth! I do now let loose
my opinion, hold it no longer: this is no fish, but an
islander, that hath lately suffered by thunderbolt.
    (*Thunder*)
Alas, the storm is come again! My best way is to
creep under his gaberdine. There is no other shelter
hereabout. Misery acquaints a man with strange
bed-fellows. I will here shroud till the dregs of the
storm be past.

[V, i, 33–57] *His work done, wrongs put right, Prospero plans to cast his final spell, a spell that will forsake the world of magic:*

Ye elves of hills, brooks, standing lakes, and groves,
 And ye that on the sands with printless foot
Do chase the ebbing Neptune, and do fly him
When he comes back; you demi-puppets that
By moonshine do the green sour ringlets make,
Whereof the ewe not bites; and you whose pastime
Is to make midnight mushrumps, that rejoice
To hear the solemn curfew; by whose aid –
Weak masters though ye be – I have bedimmed
The noontide sun, called forth the mutinous winds,
And 'twixt the green sea and the azured vault
Set roaring war; to the dread rattling thunder
Have I given fire, and rifted Jove's stout oak
With his own bolt; the strong-based promontory
Have I made shake, and by the spurs plucked up
The pine and cedar; graves at my command
Have waked their sleepers, oped, and let 'em forth
By my so potent art. But this rough magic
I here abjure; and, when I have required
Some heavenly music – which even now I do –
To work mine end upon their senses that
This airy charm is for, I'll break my staff,
Bury it certain fathoms in the earth,
And deeper than did ever plummet sound
I'll drown my book.

[III, ii, 350–72] *His plans for greatness exposed, Cardinal Wolsey comprehends the fleetingness of his achievements. With resolve he says goodbye to greatness:*

So farewell – to the little good you bear me.
Farewell, a long farewell, to all my greatness!
This is the state of man: today he puts forth
The tender leaves of hopes, to-morrow blossoms,
And bears his blushing honours thick upon him.
The third day comes a frost, a killing frost,
And when he thinks, good easy man, full surely
His greatness is a-ripening, nips his root,
And then he falls, as I do. I have ventured,
Like little wanton boys that swim on bladders,
This many summers in a sea of glory,
But far beyond my depth. My high-blown pride
At length broke under me, and now has left me
Weary and old with service, to the mercy
Of a rude stream, that must for ever hide me.
Vain pomp and glory of this world, I hate ye.
I feel my heart new open'd. O, how wretched
Is that poor man that hangs on princes' favours!
There is betwixt that smile we would aspire to,
That sweet aspect of princes, and their ruin,
More pangs and fears than wars or women have;
And when he falls, he falls like Lucifer,
Never to hope again.

[II, ii, 1–23] Arcite, banished from the kingdom, regrets only he is banished from Emilia's presence, while his cousin Palamon is free to enjoy the beauty of Emilia from his prison window:

Banished the kingdom? 'Tis a benefit,
A mercy I must thank 'em for; but banished
The free enjoying of that face I die for,
O, 'twas a studied punishment, a death
Beyond imagination; such a vengeance
That, were I old and wicked, all my sins
Could never pluck upon me. Palamon,
Thou hast the start now; thou shalt stay and see
Her bright eyes break each morning 'gainst thy
    window,
And let in life into thee; thou shalt feed
Upon the sweetness of a noble beauty,
That Nature never exceeded, nor never shall.
Good gods! what happiness has Palamon!
Twenty to one, he'll come to speak to her,
And if she be as gentle as she's fair,
I know she's his; he has a tongue will tame
Tempests, and make the wild rocks wanton.
Come what can come,
The worst is death; I will not leave the kingdom.
I know mine own is but a heap of ruins,
And no redress there. If I go, he has her.
I am resolved another shape shall make me,
Or end my fortunes. Either way, I am happy;
I'll see her, and be near her, or no more.

Besotted with Palamon, the jailer's daughter sees her folly, but resolves to enable his escape from prison in the hope she may win his affections:

Why should I love this gentleman? 'Tis odds
He never will affect me; I am base,
My father the mean keeper of his prison,
And he a prince. To marry him is hopeless;
To be his whore is witless. Out upon't!
What pushes are we wenches driven to,
When fifteen once has found us! First, I saw him;
I, seeing, thought he was a goodly man;
He has as much to please a woman in him –
If he please to bestow it so – as ever
These eyes yet looked on. Next, I pitied him,
And so would any young wench, o'my conscience,
That ever dreamed, or vowed her maidenhead
To a young handsome man. Then I loved him,
Extremely loved him, infinitely loved him;
And yet he had a cousin, fair as he too;
But in my heart was Palamon, and there,
Lord, what a coil he keeps! To hear him
Sing in an evening, what a heaven it is!
And yet his songs are sad ones. Fairer spoken
Was never gentleman. When I come in
To bring him water in a morning, first
He bows his noble body, then salutes me, thus:
'Fair, gentle maid, good morrow; may thy goodness
Get thee a happy husband.' Once he kissed me;
I loved my lips the better ten days after –
Would he would do so every day! He grieves much,

And me as much to see his misery.
What should I do, to make him know I love him?
For I would fain enjoy him. Say I ventured
To set him free? What says the law then? Thus much
For law, or kindred! I will do it;
And this night, or tomorrow, he shall love me.

[III, iv] *The jailer's daughter begins to come unhinged; lost in
the woods, her plans in disarray, Palamon seemingly dead, her
father's trust betrayed:*

I am very cold, and all the stars are out too,
  The little stars, and all, that look like aglets:
The sun has seen my folly. Palamon!
Alas, no; he's in heaven. Where am I now?
Yonder's the sea, and there's a ship; how't tumbles!
And there's a rock lies watching under water,
Now, now, it beats upon it; now, now, now,
There's a leak sprung, a sound one; how they cry!
Spoon her before the wind, you'll lose all else:
Up with a course or two, and tack about, boys.
Good night, good night, you're gone. I am very hungry.
Would I could find a fine frog; he would tell me
News from all parts o'th' world, then would I make
A carrack of a cockleshell, and sail
By east and north-east to the King of Pygmies,
For he tells fortunes rarely. Now my father,
Twenty to one, is trust up in a trice
Tomorrow morning; I'll say never a word.

[IV, ii, 1–54] *Palamon and Arcite plan to fight a duel to the death for the love of Emilia. As she compares their portraits, Emilia contemplates her conflicted heart:*

Yet I may bind those wounds up, that must open
  And bleed to death for my sake else; I'll choose,
And end their strife. Two such young handsome men
Shall never fall for me; their weeping mothers,
Following the dead cold ashes of their sons,
Shall never curse my cruelty. Good heaven,
What a sweet face has Arcite! If wise Nature
With all her best endowments, all those beauties
She sows into the births of noble bodies,
Were here a mortal woman, and had in her
The coy denials of young maids, yet doubtless
She would run mad for this man. What an eye,
Of what a fiery sparkle and quick sweetness,
Has this young prince! Here love himself sits smiling.
Just such another, wanton Ganymede
Set Jove afire with, and enforced the god
Snatch up the goodly boy, and set him by him,
A shining constellation. What a brow,
Of what a spacious majesty, he carries,
Arched like the great-eyed Juno's, but far sweeter,
Smoother than Pelops' shoulder! Fame and honour,
Me thinks, from hence, as from a promontory
Pointed in heaven, should clap their wings, and sing
To all the under world the loves and fights
Of gods, and such men near 'em. Palamon
Is but his foil, to him a mere dull shadow.
He's swarth and meagre, of an eye as heavy

As if he had lost his mother; a still temper,
No stirring in him, no alacrity,
Of all this sprightly sharpness not a smile;
Yet these that we count errors may become him;
Narcissus was a sad boy, but a heavenly.
O, who can find the bent of woman's fancy?
I am a fool, my reason is lost in me,
I have no choice, and I have lied so lewdly
That women ought to beat me. On my knees
I ask thy pardon, Palamon, thou art alone,
And only beautiful, and these the eyes,
These the bright lamps of beauty, that command
And threaten love, and what young maid dare cross
    'em?
What a bold gravity, and yet inviting,
Has this brown manly face! O, love, this only
From this hour is complexion. Lie there, Arcite,
Thou art a changeling to him, a mere gipsy,
And this the noble body. I am sotted,
Utterly lost: my virgin's faith has fled me.
For if my brother but even now had asked me
Whether I loved, I had run mad for Arcite;
Now, if my sister, more for Palamon.
Stand both together: Now, come and ask me, brother –
Alas, I know not! Ask me now, sweet sister; –
I may go look. What a mere child is fancy,
That, having two fair gods of equal sweetness,
Cannot distinguish, but must cry for both.

INDEX OF FIRST LINES

Now might I do it pat, now 'a is a-praying.
  [*Hamlet*, III, iii, 73]   61
Now, York, or never, steel thy fearful thoughts,
  [*Henry VI Part 2*, III, i, 331]   7
O all you host of heaven! O earth! What else?
  [*Hamlet*, I, v, 92]   55
O blessed breeding sun, draw from the earth
  [*Timon of Athens*, IV, iii, 1]   75
O conspiracy,
  [*Julius Caesar*, II, i, 77]   51
O God of battles, steel my soldiers' hearts;
  [*Henry V*, IV, i, 282]   49
O, my offence is rank. It smells to heaven.
  [*Hamlet*, III, iii, 36]   60
O, pardon me, thou bleeding piece of earth,
  [*Julius Caesar*, III, i, 254]   52
O Romeo, Romeo! – wherefore art thou Romeo?
  [*Romeo and Juliet*, II, ii, 33]   30
O that this too too sullied flesh would melt,
  [*Hamlet*, I, ii, 129]   54
O, were that all! I think not on my father,
  [*All's Well That Ends Well*, I, i, 78]   73
O what a rogue and peasant slave am I!
  [*Hamlet*, II, ii, 547]   56
O world, thy slippery turns! Friends now fast sworn,
  [*Coriolanus*, IV, iv, 12]   88
Peace, you ungracious clamours! Peace, rude sounds!
  [*Troilus and Cressida*, I, i, 91]   65
Poor naked wretches, wheresoe'er you are,
  [*King Lear*, III, iv, 28]   80